Authentic, Aligned, and Abundant

YOUR TRIPLE-A GUIDE TO CREATING YOUR MAGNIFICENT LIFE

DIANE HILL

Praise for Diane Hill & *Authentic, Aligned, and Abundant*

"Di is just fabulous. She made me reevaluate who I was and what I wanted. I have a clearer vision of who I am and what my purpose is. She made me realise how fabulous life is and gave me tools to create whatever I wanted in life. Thank you for always being there for me and being only a phone call away. I would recommend her to anyone who wants to lead a purposeful life."

– Taryn Vollmer

"Working with Di has literally changed my life. I was stuck in a rut for so long, but her process and guidance made me realise this was not the way life needed to be. In one year, I bought my dream house, regained control of my career, started gym and meditating regularly, and lost some weight without a horrible diet. She made me believe in myself and the process. I would recommend EVERYONE give her course a try. You only have one life, and you had better own it."

- Natalie Stephan

"My journey with Di has been life-changing. We got deep, we got uncomfortable, but I came out lighter with a huge heartfelt understanding of Why. I now have all the tools I need to keep me feeling confident, feeling worthy, feeling abundant, feeling in control—and the best gift she gave me is that I have created an incredible life that I love living."

- Clare Sirin

"Di has poured her heart and soul into learning how to deal with life's many lessons. She had shared her knowledge, tenacity and infectious positive energy with me on numerous occasions and workshops. I highly recommend spending some valuable time with yourself and Di. You won't regret it!"

- Jenny Kjellqvist

"Having Di as part of my support structure was inspirational! Her enthusiasm is contagious, leaving you feeling light and positive. Di offers a unique perspective and delivers wonderful results."

- Juanita Miller

"Di taught me that the greatest shifts are self-compassion, self-awareness, and self-love. I learned to give myself permission to have time out and to fill my own cup, as well as practicing abundance and not coming from a place of lack. I know that I am enough and that it is ok to take time for yourself to do what makes your heart happy! I now have more confidence, acceptance and gratitude for who I am and what I have achieved. Di showed me that perfection is an impossible state to aim for!"

- Lorna Wright Jones

"Thank you, Di, for sharing your story. It will resonate deeply with so many women who have lost their path and are seeking answers. This book is a truly valuable guide to help truth-seekers wake up and live their best 10-out-of-10 life. No matter where you are in life, this is one of those books you'll want to come back to time and again."

- Sanae Floyd

"A must-read for anyone who wants to live with purpose! Beautifully and authentically written, Di describes her own journey of self-discovery, and through this, she shares easy-to-use techniques to create the life you were meant to live! After reading the book, I am continuing to discover who I truly am and this book is my companion on my own journey of self-discovery."

- Laurie Jimerson

Authentic, Aligned, and Abundant:
Your Triple-A Guide To Creating Your Magnificent Life

Aviva Publishing
Lake Placid, NY
(518) 523-1320
www.AvivaPubs.com

This work depicts actual events in the life of the author as truthfully as recollection permits and/or can be verified by research. The names of some individuals have been changed to respect their privacy. Every attempt has been made to source all quotes properly.

For additional copies or bulk purchases, address all inquiries to:
www.dihillempowermentcoaching.com
www.authenticalignedandabundant.com

Editor: Duo Storytelling
Publishing Coach: Christine Gail
Cover Design and Interior Layout: Fusion Creative Works

ISBN: 978-1-63618-171-4
Library of Congress Control Number: 2022900357

10 9 8 7 6 5 4 3 2 1

First Edition, 2022

Printed in the United States of America

Dedication

This book is dedicated to all humans in the hope that you, too, will choose to live from conscious awareness, from a place of truth and love to help bring peace and harmony to not only your world, but for the greater good, so we can evolve and live from a place of love—the way we were designed to.

The Journey Home - By Diane Hill

There's a disconnect
From what I want with who I am
I am scared, alone, only my thoughts and I
Am I the only one?

I fear regret, what a waste that would be
I am hiding—from others, the world but most of all myself

I feel angry, but there's a power inside
I am jealous, but there's a desire inside
I stand in darkness, but there's glimpses of light
I feel sad, but there's moments of joy

The energy of frustration that circles inside makes me want to shout at the top of my voice,
Run until I can't no more,
Cry until my tears have run out
I curl myself into a ball, what have I become?

I'm being a victim, but that's a lie
I'm telling myself I'm lost when actually I'm found

There's a voice that's getting louder, so loud I can't ignore it no more
It's somewhere deep inside of me
It's the voice of my soul, pleading to listen more
That voice, it resides in my heart
That is my home

I travel down from my head to my heart and start listening
I am home, I am at peace
I am one with the spirit that lives inside of me
I am one with the enthusiasm that beats like a drum inside
I trust myself, I love myself, I know exactly what I want

I dare to listen within
I dare to unleash the power inside
I rise up to meet myself and fall in love with the miraculous creation
I am
A limitless, powerful creator, a divine being—the same as the universe itself
I can create the life of my dreams

I choose power over anger
Desire over jealousy
Light over darkness
Joy over sadness
I have returned to my home

Contents

Introduction

Are you feeling like I did? Lost, scared, fearful? Possibly resentful or angry? Wondering if life is just passing you by? Is the person you portray to the outside world completely different from the one inside?

I see you . . . because I was once you. I've walked your walk. I know what it's like to wonder if this is what life is meant to be and if it's going to disappear in the blink of an eye. I know you're afraid that time is running out and that you're not living life to your highest potential, purposefully, and with joy. You might project a smiling face to the outside world, pretending that everything is okay, but in truth, you're borderline miserable and wondering why you don't feel that unbridled joy. I know you feel that uneasy disconnection between your external life and what that increasingly loud inner voice truly desires. You know—that voice you try to ignore, which questions your lack of happiness and why it feels impossible to get what you want. Who is that voice anyway? Are you hoping it might go away?

The fantastic news is, you're in the right place. That's how I used to feel, and I want to share how you can stop being a slave to this. I never believed that the elusive "happy life" everyone else had was available to me. I spent my time comparing, not feeling good enough, and ruminating about my past decisions. Worst of all, I was scared that I wouldn't live my life with true meaning or fulfilment, resulting in becoming an unhappy, negative old woman who was way past her sell-by date and who was missing the opportunity at creating an incredible life.

Life operates at speed, and no, you're not getting any younger—although this book may make you feel like it! You've picked up this book because you think you're the only one that feels scared while everyone else has it worked out. However, know that on some level, everyone is frightened of sitting on that rocking chair when they're old, being full of regret for the things they didn't do, the dreams that remained dreams, and the frustration of not being able to turn back the clock. You're here because you know, deep down, you want to get somewhere that evokes those feelings of freedom, peace, calm, joy, and completeness. You think the external world will bring those feelings in the form of relationships, money, a promotion at work, or holidays. But the high you get is only temporary and you quickly revert to those underlying feelings of inadequacy, judgment, irritation, and annoyance at being unable to hold onto those feelings you so desperately want.

That place you're striving to get to, where life flows effortlessly and magically, a place of ease and happiness, isn't a destination. The place that feels out of reach to you is actually a feeling you want to experience. A feeling of inner peace, relief, love, acceptance, complete joy, and freedom to live in accordance with who you truly are—that inner voice, your soul.

Your only job is to work out how to create that feeling. You can do this by consciously choosing to live as your authentic self and knowing why you want what you want. This is you daring to step into your truth, knowing what your heart's desires are, and cleverly designing your life, deliberately and intentionally, to create the abundance you were born deserving. Those high-vibrational feelings of peace, freedom, and happiness are already within you. This is what the universe wants you to discover, what the journey of life is all about, what this book wants for you: to find the limitless freedom to joyfully be yourself within you.

You have everything you need to create your best life. It might be a rocky path as you unearth your truth, full of dead ends and wrong turns. Don't waste your valuable time being miserable and procrastinating. Ask yourself: if not now, when? Remind yourself that your ascension to living your life in alignment from a place of authenticity is your path to "unbecoming" your most awesome self.

Your self-realisation might be a gradual, beautiful unfoldment, like a flower slowly coming into bloom. Or it might just take a single moment to wake you up to the freedom within. Discovering your true self is a process, but after reading this book, you will never revert to your old self. You can never unsee what you've seen. You will be too aware, challenging your thoughts and behaviour, allowing you to transcend the old version of yourself and live in a place of consciousness, love, and authenticity. Sit, relish, and read. Buy a beautiful journal in which to make notes as you go and allow yourself to lean into the pure enjoyment of discovering the potent and powerful knowledge of who you truly are.

Over the last four years, I have gone from feeling miserable and frustrated, blaming others for where I am in life, to feeling free, happy, purposeful, and resolute in the belief that anything is possible. I revere and respect my one precious life, and I will not live it with regret. I will not turn around when I am ninety and realize I had forgotten to live my life, the one divinely bestowed to me. Instead, I choose to live in harmony with my soul—the only voice worth listening to—and make decisions from where my soul resides, my heart, with absolute faith that this will bring the high vibrational feelings I seek.

What to Expect

This book is about finding out who you are, deep down in your soul, so you have the skills to create the very best version of yourself and live your best life. For most, this will remain a mystery. They just try to get through their lives whilst forever trying to ignore thoughts about what they believed it could be. For others, the realization may come much later in life, as they become aware of time disappearing and the fear of regret looms. Consider yourself blessed that you've picked up this book now.

This book provides a roadmap of how to consciously empower yourself so you can take yourself to a place where you effortlessly curate your best life. As you unpeel the layers of armour you've unknowingly built up, you'll truly align with your soul and feel that sense of self, calm, peace, love, and joy. Instead of reacting to situations, you'll respond with conscious awareness and curiosity. You'll become more objective and forgiving towards yourself, others, and situations. You'll feel more ease and acceptance with unshakable self-belief as you lean into and trust your soul's desires. You'll feel joy and excitement knowing that life doesn't have to be one of default, nor does it have to be happening to you. Instead, you can discover the innate ability and power to design your dream life and experience it happening for you!

How This Book Is Organized

This book is broken down into three parts for you. Each is full of exercises and thought-provoking questions to take you on this incredible journey of discovering and living your truth.

Part 1—Authenticity

You can't be aligned with who you are meant to be until you peel back the layers of who you think you are. Let's rewind the tape and look back at your childhood to understand why you see the world the way you do. I'll show you how you've been living someone else's life and not taking responsibility, and how your beliefs and attitudes block you from creating your very best life. I'll show you why you've feared stepping into your power and how to undo those self-sabotaging behaviours.

Part 2—Alignment

Now that you know your truth and who you actually are, I'll show you how to uncover what it is you truthfully want and why, so your inner and outer worlds are aligned allowing you to create a life you love. I'll teach you techniques to listen to your soul and manifest what you want.

Part 3—Abundance

When you find true alignment with your soul and know what you desire, I'll show you how to cleverly curate this abundance in your life by rewiring the future version of yourself. Finally, you will learn that stepping into your power and living a life of intention with limitless ability allows you to create the magnificent life you deserve.

Tools and Techniques

My hope is that, from reading this book and completing the exercises, you will have a giant toolbox of ideas from which to choose. These will help you navigate your unconscious crisis and burst out the other side. To unleash who you are, meet and fall in love with the most amazing version of yourself, so you can live a life of freedom, peace, and joy all from a place of love.

Remember you are loved, approved, and supported just the way you are. You are a perfect creation, cut from the same cloth as the universe itself. You are —an energetic, emotional, and spiritual being having a physical experience. Let's bring your physical human and soul together so you can experience your most magnificent life, which is your birth right. Make the decision, right now, to step into the truth of who you are, whatever gets thrown in your way. You owe it to yourself because, as Oprah Winfrey says, "You know deep down what it is, because you know what it's not." That's why you've picked up this book.

PART 1

AUTHENTICITY

1

What Do You Actually Want?

"Awakening to our authentic selves
as love leads us to letting go of who we think we
should be and embracing who we actually are."

— Debra L Reble PhD

Up until now, I'm going to guess you're living in a "push/pull" life where sometimes life is full of joy and you're happy, but often not so. You still haven't quite figured out what you really want or how to get it, and more importantly, you haven't worked out how to effortlessly feel the joy and freedom you know deep down is available. You just can't seem to hold on to it, even when you feel those feelings. Why do those feelings only come now and again and then you're plunged back into feeling the disconnect and fear that life is not quite what you want? Let me tell you now, you will never create those magical feelings of freedom and the magnificent life you desire *unless you discover who you really are.*

Waking Up

For approximately five years, I experienced a long, drawn-out midlife crisis. To the outside world, everything appeared great, but inside I was miserable and scared. I silently blamed everyone else for where I was in life. Jealous of others' supposedly fabulous lives, looks, attitude, confidence, figures, achievements, careers, parenting, knowledge, life experiences, and relationships. Nothing I did felt quite good enough. I was angry inside but had no idea why, and felt sad with a serious lack of self-worth underneath that smiley exterior.

I resented myself for what I had or hadn't done—what I hadn't gone for, achieved, or let go of. At the same time, I felt completely stunned, with nervous energy racing around me, fearful the future would be the same and I'd never reach the true potential inside me. I was in no-man's-land, pivoting between the past and future, never embracing the present.

You would have never known this of course, because I presented a very different person than what I felt inside. This is something many of us are extremely good at, and it is the cause of much internal misery and frustration.

In November 2017, I returned to the UK—my home country—for a week, leaving my husband and three children behind. It was the first time in nine years I had been on my own overnight. I felt a strange combination of nausea, fear, and guilt about going, but also excitement, joy, and *relief* at the freedom and adventure that lay ahead of me. The quieted headspace, time, and energy to lean into a life that once was.

That week was a life-altering moment for me. I didn't go on a spiritual retreat, meet a psychic, or do psychedelic drugs, but I slowly found myself once again. Like a light's dimmer switch slowly being turned up. In my newfound headspace, I caught glimpses of Di once again, amongst the noise, chaos, and energy of London. I allowed *myself* to come up to the surface once again, taking it all in. Energy like I hadn't felt in years coursed through my veins as I breathed in the city where I'd once forged out a career. I didn't want to miss a moment of those high-vibe feelings of independence, freedom, and unlimited potential. I walked to the beat of my own drum, with a mind so clear that I didn't stop smiling for a week—although the fear of this unbridled happiness disappearing again quietly lurked in the background of my mind.

Before I knew it, my time was up and that familiar, heavy feeling in my gut returned once more. Over the years, I had become skilled at living with this uncomfortable feeling and plastering on a happy face, but I still would rather have not had it. Why was it back? Was it guilt? Was it the realization that my day-to-day life didn't evoke those same high-vibe feelings? Was it fear that life would revert to normal, and this sacred week would become an ever-distant memory? To acknowledge that I wasn't living with true happiness and to my highest potential was something I was extremely scared of. I was delighted Di was still in there, but at the same time, I had a deep-seated fear of what lay ahead. In the process of coming alive, I grieved for what I'd allowed to die.

"How many people are trapped in their everyday habits: part numb, part frightened, part indifferent? To have a better life we must keep choosing how we are living."

— Albert Einstein

Over the next few months, I couldn't shake this feeling of having rediscovered myself again, but real life had me feeling trapped. Like a caged bird, I flapped about, trying to make myself happy whilst ignoring that ever-present heavy feeling in my gut—the feeling that things weren't quite right, but I couldn't put my finger on what or why. I distracted myself with family life, friends, exercise, cooking, shopping, Netflix—anything to stop me from feeling my true anger, fear, and sadness. Life felt out of my control, I didn't know what I wanted, and time kept passing.

When I allowed myself to think about it, I realised the person I was most angry with was myself. I was angry at never having a successful career or using my degree or subsequent qualifications. I was angry with my negative mindset, limited financial independence, and knowledge of how to manage money effectively. I had become lazy about looking after myself and stating what I needed. I had allowed my dreams to be put on the back burner. At the same time, I was on edge and fired up. I was acutely aware of the "me" inside, and I wanted to live my life to the fullest. I didn't want an "ok" life full of the odd peaks of joy from something external. I was determined to find a way through this, to discover the joy I knew lay within, I just didn't know how.

The universe listened and provided signs for me to wake up. I read personal development books as I tried to make sense of my feelings. I hired a life coach to try to work out what I wanted, and I started meditating to calm my frenetic brain and clarify what made me tick. I made the choice to speak up for myself, thinking, What's the worst that could happen? This caused some disagreements, but I was done ignoring myself and feeling dissatisfied. I had no idea I was on a path of awakening to my soul—who I really was, deep down inside.

In September 2018, I visited New York, my favourite city in the world. I love the energy, the noise, the smell, the buildings, the people, the gritty realness of it, the belief that anything is possible. A city where dreams are made—and often come true. Even songs tell us this is the case. In New York, I felt that sense of peace again, excitement and joy coursing around my veins.

If London had gently prodded me, New York literally shook me awake and went on to drastically change my life. That week springboarded me into discovering who I really was and what my purpose was—birthing a business that would help others discover who they really were, and writing this book. What happened then was nothing less than magical. Within the twenty-four hours after my plane departed from my home city, I encountered my own name seven times. Seven times. I never usually came across my name like that.

"When your highest priority is to follow the guidance of your heart and soul, you'll hear your inner wisdom."

— Dr John Demartini

On the plane, I started reading a crime thriller novel set in New York. One of the characters was a middle-aged secretary named Diane. Okay, nothing odd there, just mild annoyance that Diane was a suitable name for a woman of age. I turned on the in-flight movies and watched Book Club. It featured another character called Diane, this time also played by Diane Keaton. Her character was middle-aged, divorced, and had lived her entire existence for her children. She was frazzled, regretful, stuck, and bored. I didn't like her. Mostly because it made me afraid that I might end up like her.

On my connecting flight, I watched the HBO series Divorce, which had a vivacious character called Diane. I felt vague amusement at how many times I'd now heard my name. This Diane had a second husband, whom she depended on (my husband is also my second), and a champagne lifestyle. I liked her; she was strong, crazy, ridiculous, powerful, and said what she thought. Wasn't that who I was becoming? Wasn't she being her real self? Maybe my name wasn't so bad after all.

I had time for one more quick movie before I landed: an easy comedy called Life of the Party. The protagonist, Deanna, was a downtrodden housewife whose husband had left her, so she went back to college to finish her degree, with all the fun of being free from any responsibility. This brought up uncomfortable grief and sadness about how much time had passed since my youth, what I'd done since, and whether I would ever feel those limitless feelings of fun and freedom ever again.

The next morning, I jumped on an early train into Manhattan, happily basking in the energy of the New York accents around me. The city had me beaming, completely at peace. The lady next to me was talking to her friend on her cell phone—Diane, of course. The lady was consoling Diane about a failed relationship and assuring her that all would be okay. Now I was getting a little freaked out. I never hear my name, but in less than a day, I'd already heard it six times.

I got off the train and started to walk with enthusiastic determination to not miss a thing, inhaling the energy and the feelings of joy and freedom. I walked down to the memorial site where the World Trade Center once stood, feeling the sombre energy in the air. Hundreds of people were there paying their respects, showing love, support, and empathy to those that had lost their lives that day. I walked over to one of the two square, waist-high plinths—the footprint perimeter of each tower—and looked over to see a never-ending waterfall in the middle. I jostled myself to the front and began reading the names of the nearly three thousand people who had died that day, elegantly carved into the stone plinth. Right in front of me was the name "Dianne T. Signer and her unborn child".

Tears flowed at the combination of sadness and rage at what had happened, followed by complete fear as I tried to imagine what she had experienced. I stumbled away, shocked at how deeply I felt it all. When I reached the subway, I openly cried once again as I realized that I had heard my name again. It was now so loud in my head that I didn't know what to think. I caught my breath as mild panic took over. Who was talking to me? Was it the universe? God? My inner self?

As I walked over the Brooklyn Bridge to Manhattan, navigating my way among other tourists and the souvenir-sellers, looking up to the sky, I said quietly but firmly "Okay, I'm listening. Whoever you are, I've heard you, what is it I have to do?" I took a deep breath and strode on.

That was it. That was my lightbulb moment, and a sign from something far bigger than me to finally start listening to that voice getting increasingly louder inside of me.

Later, I realized I only heard this voice because it was the first time in my life that I was open to hearing it. I was no longer receiving confused fuzzy signals I couldn't make sense of. Finally, the airwaves were open, and I was tuned into receiving what was being transmitted. That day, the day I walked half a marathon across Manhattan, I chose to listen to that voice. I was going to start living according to what felt good and right to me, what my heart and soul wanted. I had been so busy living according to who I thought "I should be" and being guided by my head that I had pushed away the one voice that so desperately wanted to be heard. My sign to wake up and live my truth had come. If I didn't owe it to myself, I at least owed it to my departed namesake.

The Empowerment Process

"The privilege of a lifetime is to find out who you truly are."

— Carl Jung

The process of empowerment is about awakening yourself to the truth living inside you—the truth that's waiting to get out. It shows you how to take yourself back to that vibration of love, peace, acceptance, and freedom that you were designed to live from. Give yourself a hug and tell yourself how much you love yourself as you honour and respect the disconnection you've felt between your inner and external worlds. Perhaps it was a specific event like I experienced, or you've reached this juncture from a place of pain, but you don't need a major life trauma to shake you awake. Trauma with a little "t" can be just as impactful, such as a lifetime of feeling inadequate or unloved but knowing innately there must be a different way.

Why Commitment Is Key

"Be who you are and find yourself so you can be your own person and enjoy life with no regret."

— Bonnie Zackson Koury

This process of becoming yourself might be unsettling as you realize you've not been living your life how you were meant to. It requires you to go within and do some soul searching. It might touch raw nerves, unearthing feelings you don't want to feel, as you look back at the past and thoughts you judge yourself for. You might need to let go of people or situations that hold you out of integrity and no longer serve your greatness. This might trigger feelings of fear because humans have an innate need for connection. Setting boundaries, saying no, or challenging others' expectations of you might feel difficult because we fear rejection. To discover the person you were always meant to be, you must make decisions from your heart, from a place of love—not from your mind or what you think you should be doing.

A commitment to evolving into the best version of yourself can take time, effort, patience, and most of all, intent. It's too easy to just be interested, then give up when the process isn't easy and convenient. This is about you making a conscious choice to live a different way. This is about finding out who you really are, being willing to unpeel the layers, and processing the nonsense holding you back, so you can live with the joy, freedom, and ease you crave.

What Freedom Is

Most people think freedom is being free from limits, constrictions, worry, or lack. This isn't correct. To be free, you just have to live in accordance with your higher self, that voice inside. Freedom is already within you. It's a higher order. It's your birth right. We are free already. You have infinite energy to express who you are deep down, if you let it. You just need to find what creates it for you. Nothing external can grant this; it's an inside job. Therefore, you need to be conscious of your authentic nature, use this self-awareness to choose what it is you want, what feels good and believe that you have the power to create your own reality. Choice is a function of expanded awareness, where you choose to make decisions from a higher level of thought. The empire state of mind resides inside your heart.

"Self-care is not self-indulgence, it is self-preservation."

— Audre Lorde

Creating Time for This Work

This is your time. Time to do what you need to do to find yourself, heal yourself, and discover your truth. It is not selfish or arrogant to put yourself first, whatever society tells us. Those are just judgements stemming from the fear of feeling unworthy or not deserving. Demonstrate self-love by investing your time and giving yourself permission to do this work. If this creates uncomfortable feelings in you, ask yourself why. Do you not deserve to discover what is divinely yours and live your best life?

"If you don't design your own life,
chances are you'll fall into someone else's plan. And guess
what they have planned for you? Not much."

— Jim Rohn

Great lives don't just happen, they are intentionally created from a deep-seated knowledge of who you are and what you must do to live to your highest potential. I invite you to do the work and trust that it is golden on the other side. Giving yourself time to be present and work on yourself is one of life's greatest gifts. It says you matter: you value yourself, respect yourself, and have a deep sense of self-worth. You must prioritize and love yourself; you will never create the incredible reality you want any other way. Commit to yourself to reading the chapters, contemplating, and looking within. Every day, tell yourself you are going to do it. Commitment starts with you changing your thoughts, not your habits.

"You need to make a commitment,
and once you make it, then life will give you some answers."

— Les Brown

The way you ascend into who you really are may not make sense to those around you, but to get what you want, you have to stay focused on creating it. Otherwise, you will get distracted and time will disappear. Commitment takes courage, respect, and discipline. It involves being assertive, speaking up for what you want, and living from intuition and love as you take back your power. This can be terrifying if you've lived according to who you thought you should be or to others' expectations, but know that you are safe, loved, and that living from a place of truth is the only way to freedom.

Wasting time by procrastinating means you will judge yourself because you feel you're not accomplishing what you think you should. This will create feelings of inadequacy, which stops you from working on yourself. Simply put, you won't believe what you want is available to you or that you deserve it. It's a form of self-sabotage that keeps you safe and small instead of reaching your highest potential. We do this to avoid failure because we tie how we feel about ourselves to what we achieve. Society sees failure as a negative thing, so it's better not to try. When we do new and unfamiliar things, it feels scary, but it's just the disconnection between the conscious and subconscious part of your brain. This uncomfortable feeling is temporary, but you can push through it by telling yourself why you're doing this, and then it will become familiar. If you find yourself procrastinating, acknowledge what's really going on and what you're trying to avoid. Then practice some self-forgiveness and pour some love and grace on yourself.

Write down the times of the week on a calendar that you are going to set aside to work on the personal up-levelling of your awesome self. The more you show up for yourself, the more the universe will show up for you.

Saying What You Truly Feel

"People start to heal the moment they are heard."

— Cheryl Richardson

An important part of this process is to be honest with yourself about your true feelings. Suppressing them is where the problems start. When you express your true emotions and are heard, you instantly feel better. This starts to physically and energetically release what you've been holding in for so long, which has been stopping you being your most awesome self. Feelings and emotions are part of a chemical process that is meant to be fully felt, processed, and released. However, we live in a world where it can be scary to voice how we really feel, so we instead deny our emotions and push them down. Physically, our bodies know exactly when to expel things that affect us, so think of this process as doing the same with your emotions and beliefs.

The first step of becoming your best self and discovering your authenticity is to release the energy of old emotional wounds by saying them aloud or writing them down. You might want to say or write:

- "I'm bored with my life"
- "I don't like being a parent"
- "I don't like responsibility"
- "I regret my past"
- "I'm not thin enough/good enough/rich enough"

- "I don't like my partner"
- "I hate myself"
- "I hate my job"
- "I don't like my house"
- "I'm a failure and racked with guilt"
- "I feel trapped"
- "I'm such a bad person"

Go on, write it all down—even the things you're scared to say to yourself for fear of judgement. Now ask why you feel this way. Those negative feelings are not weak or something to hide away from. They are there to help you learn and grow. I will show you how to process these feelings, release and transcend them, and recognize that holding onto them stops you from being your best, most amazing self.

What Do You Really Want?

Dream Life Exercise:

What would a 10-out-of-10 dream life look like to you? Think of the various areas (domains) of your life:

- Career/vocation
- Family and friends
- Personal relationships
- Wellness (including leisure and social)
- Wealth
- Personal development and education
- Spirituality or contribution
- Physical environment

Write down your dreams, desires, and ideas about these different areas in the present tense—for example, "I meditate each day", "I improve myself with personal development courses", or "I always have enough money to enjoy my life". Envision every area of it. What do you look like? What are you wearing? What is the temperature? Who is with you? What feelings are evoked in you as you think about your dream life that makes you feel enthusiastic and excited? Who do you want to be? What do you need to do to become that person? Do you truly want these things or is it to satisfy others? Keep asking, adding, and rewriting as you go. This is a living document!

Ask what has stopped you from acting in these areas before or is standing in the way of this dream life. Relationships, time, money, past beliefs, resources, friends, parents, society? What are you scared of?

Now ask yourself what proof you have that creating the life of your dreams isn't available to you.

Now list ten reasons why you must create this magnificent life and ten consequences of not achieving it.

Enjoy this beautiful, indulgent process and be open to signs around you as you discover what you want and what feels right. You don't have to write this in one go. It might not come naturally to you, especially if you are used to doing what everyone else thinks you should do. Welcome any changes or things you're scared of that you think may excite you. Maybe that's different sports or hobbies you've never tried before, a different relationship than the one you're in now, learning new skills, or applying for a different job. Just enjoy the fantasy of this dream life. Forgive yourself as you chop and change; that's the beauty of the human experience.

When You Don't Know What You Want

There may be such a massive disconnect between your reality (the external world) and what your inner self wants, you no longer know what you want, creating a mental fog that makes you feel lost and fearful. If this is you, try this exercise to help get some clarity.

Open a clean page in your journal. On the left-hand side, write the eight areas of your life leaving space between each, and write down all the stuff you don't want.

For example:

- I don't want to be on my own.
- I don't want to be poor.
- I don't want to feel rushed.
- I don't want to feel overwhelmed.
- I don't want my boss to overlook me.
- I don't want my kids to ignore me.
- I don't want to feel unaccomplished.
- I don't want to feel unloved.
- I don't want to feel rejected.

Then on the opposite page, write the exact opposite of all the things you said you don't want. Reading them back, what do those things make you feel? You'll know by how you feel in your gut. Is it dark and heavy (no, you don't really want it), or is it light and flowy (yes, it's right!)? Can you weave these into your dream life to lay the foundations of what you truly want?

Exercise: Fifty things that make me happy

Write down a long, indulgent list of fifty things that make you happy. You don't need to do this in one go, so enjoy the process! Spend time journaling, and be mindful of ideas that come to you when you are doing something completely different. Maybe it will be as small as getting a coffee with a friend, bedtime hugs with your children, or freshly cut grass. Or maybe it will be as big as travelling around the world or delivering a huge project at work. For each one, ask yourself why this makes you happy. Do these make your soul sing or are you doing these things because you think you should?

For example:

Running: ***Why? It pumps me full of energy, I've been out in nature, I'm looking after my body, I listen to music I love. It fills my soul (versus I should because I'll become unfit and put weight on).***

Spending time with friends: ***Why? Because I love the connection and laughter we have together (versus fearing missing out).***

Now look at your life. How often do you do these things that make you happy? Why don't you do more of them? Do you feel guilty when you do them? Are you worthy enough to spend time doing things that make you happy?

What about all the things you spend your time doing? This includes time-wasting, procrastinating, scrolling on social media, mindlessly messaging people, dwelling and ruminating on things, as well as the have-to's—the usual day-to-day stuff, such as cleaning, cooking, travelling, or family life. How does this compare with your fifty things list? Can you incorporate more of your want-to's into your life along with the have-to's?

"The two most important days of your life are the one when you were born and the day you find out why."

— Mark Twain

You are already starting to create a picture of what you want. However, it's only possible to get to where you want to be with a clear understanding of why you're doing it. This provides the fuel for your determination to reach your dreams. Knowing your "why" is the driving force behind everything you do and gives you purpose and motivation to reach your desires. Keep asking why until you get to the root of the driving force behind your motivation.

Okay, that's a lot, but you're on your way! You've booked your ticket (this book), you've boarded your flight (you've committed), and you're ready for take-off. Buckle up, my love, and enjoy the excitement! You're strapped in with a safety belt of love and support. Embrace the turbulence, the inflight movie of your life, and relax into the freedom you're destined for.

2

Why You Believe What You Want Isn't Available to You

"When you think everything is someone else's fault, you suffer a lot. When you realise everything only springs from yourself, you will learn both peace and joy."

— Dalai Lama

The Four Stages of Spiritual Growth

Now that you have a handle on what it is you want, it's important to understand why you haven't created it in your life yet. Know that this process of discovering your authenticity is a lifestyle choice. It is an ever-evolving eye-opening journey, with twists and turns along the way. The path to living in accordance with your highest potential is intertwined with the four stages of spiritual growth—all so you can arrive at that destination, that feeling you want to reach: freedom.

According to renowned author and Reverend Michael Beckwith, the four stages of spiritual growth demonstrate how we develop as individuals. Many of us start from a place where we feel that life is happening *"to* us", but as we grow we feel life happening *"for* us". From here we experience spiritual growth, with life happening *"through* us" and eventually *"as* us" as we seek to understand and deeply acknowledge that we are all connected energetically as one collective consciousness. One energy, cut from the same energy of the universe—the energy of love. Before we go into the energetics of creating what you want, you must first understand why you haven't got it.

Stage 1—Victimhood

This first stage has been manufactured by society so that most people feel as if life is happening with little or no control. Life feels as if it is happening *to* us, and we just receive and accept our experiences. This is how much of the world operates—and where I used to be, before I woke up. In this stage, we are on the receiving end of situations or challenges and unconsciously react to them with little thought or awareness—i.e., the physical environment controlling our experience. This is when we are reactionary to situations, triggered by people or events, and lack awareness because we don't know our authentic selves. Whilst you have a desire for things to be different, you feel stuck and powerless, not believing it is possible to create the life you want. It's a place of little to no responsibility, where it's everyone else's fault instead of ours. We blame others for where we are in life and what we are missing out on.

This is you unconsciously going through life, accepting "as is" based on your individual experience, letting the outside (external) world determine how you feel.

My lack of a successful career wasn't *my* fault; I just didn't attend a good enough school, nor was I given the correct career advice. My poor money-management skills were because I'd never been taught to be financially independent. I hadn't realised my dreams because I didn't believe they were available to me. These are all indications of being a victim.

Much of the human race operates this way because we haven't been taught to live another way. The world is set up like this, pointing fingers and blaming others because it's easier to do this than take responsibility for our own actions, words, or deeds. We live with our own unique perception of life, formed from stories we've heard and experiences we've had—often through a lens of lack. It is impossible to create a fulfilling and abundant life from this place because you don't believe you have the power to do so or that it is available to you. That is why taking responsibility is the first step of growing spiritually into the second stage: empowerment.

"You can't go back and change the beginning but you can start where you are at and change the ending."

— C S Lewis

Stage 2—Empowerment

The second stage of spiritual awakening is when you begin to wake up and realise you *do* have control over your thoughts, actions, and deeds. It is an exciting and powerful stage. You become aware of the abundance that is available and divinely given to you, and you realise the power to create your best life is in your hands. You acknowledge that life happens *for* you, and this excites, fuels, and drives you to become more self-aware, conscious, and open to all the potential that exists in the universe. You no longer act like a powerless victim, operating in the confines of your own mind, and instead take responsibility for where you are in life.

This stage can be painful but ultimately life-changing because it is so transformative. *Once you have woken up, you can never go back to sleep*. It can bring up feelings of regret—or darker emotions such as shame, guilt, anger, or fear—to accept you haven't lived authentically, you've renounced responsibility, and you've actually enabled or created things in your life that didn't serve your greatness. As you are challenged by circumstances that you originally perceived to be beyond your control, you may feel inadequate or have fear that resources are too scarce to create what you want. Reading this book, working through the exercises, and understanding that all your challenges are beautiful lessons will allow you to go deeper and pull out the nonsense that is holding you back.

Stage 3—Surrender

When you reach this point, aware of your power to manifest what you want, acceptance follows as you release the need to have control over your destiny. This stage of spiritual growth is where life happens *through* you. You no longer feel the need to grind things out. Instead, you'll be accepting, present, grateful, and let things come with divine timing. You will have an unwavering faith that the universe has your back, supporting you as you surrender to your life's path. You have mastered your mindset and no longer have to consciously apply yourself, easily creating a life in accordance with your soul's desires.

When we accept life as happening *through* us, we feel peace. It's natural and light. In fact, it feels incredible and magical, as if something far greater than us is guiding us along in life. This is when we say we are "in flow", or things just come easy to us because we are in alignment with our soul and what our hearts want. We let go of any need for control and start trusting in the process and our connection to the bigger picture, the universe, the source, or God, so that life can flow through us. To truly surrender is awe-inspiring. The relief washes over you and any fear you feel dissolves.

Life is made up of many domains, and your path to spiritual awakening isn't uniform across them. You might feel incredibly empowered or even be in the surrender stage in one area of your life (such as your career or physical health) but still remain in the victimhood stage in other areas of your life (such as relationships or finances). We also pivot up and down between these different stages as we create new situations, prompting us to challenge our responses to things we still need to heal from. Self-awareness and acceptance that we are exactly where we need to be helps us appreciate that we heal in layers. *This* is what allows you to remain conscious in your thoughts, actions, and deeds. The more you practice awareness of what you're being shown to heal from, the more you'll create what you want in your life.

Your freedom comes from listening to your soul, as opposed to driven by your mind. The more we attune to this, the more we step ever closer to the final stage of spiritual growth: awakening.

Stage 4—Awakening

As we allow who we truly are to unfold, we understand and appreciate that we are all part of a bigger experience. We accept that we are energetic beings (albeit in a very dense form) connected as one collective consciousness. We respect that we are the same as the infinite creative force of the universe. This is expressed as life happening as "me" or "I am" because we are all made by the very same thing as the essence of the universe—energy. You are a unique expression of this force.

This stage is rarely available to us, as we so often become distracted by the outside world, but good examples of enlightened individuals include Gandhi, the Dalai Lama, Buddha, Eckhart Tolle, and Deepak Chopra.

Taking Responsibility

"Stop pointing fingers and placing
blame on others. Your life can only change
to the degree that you accept responsibility for it."

— Dr Steve Maraboli

As you will learn, the only person that can make you feel empowered and create your best life is you. You help yourself. You're no longer a child, and your job on this planet is to strive to live to your highest potential. You won't get what you want when you believe where you are in life is everyone else's fault. When you release the need to blame, shame, and make excuses, this is the beginning of your authentic journey. Now you start to edge towards empowerment and manifesting the life of your dreams.

We think manifesting is just creating all the shiny stuff you want—money, promotions, relationships, cars, holidays, and so on—but you are actually creating your reality all the time. We so often create from lack, scarcity, and fear, driven by how we see life as victims of circumstance. You need to open your eyes to this and know that you ultimately created it all. You are 100 percent responsible for everything that has happened to you, you just don't believe it. Your job on the path to becoming the magnificent being you were always designed to be is to accept this, heal the emotional wounds and programming imprinted on you, and be brave enough to live in accordance with who you authentically are. This is what will evoke feelings of freedom.

Why We Hate to Take Responsibility

The best example of humans not taking responsibility is little children arguing. My children love a good argument, and they desperately try to prove their point and win back any power they feel is slipping from their hands—i.e., childhood dramas. They want something their way, they hate their opinion being challenged, or they want something the other has. So, they fight. Sometimes verbally, but it can get physical. It's enough to drive any parent crazy, afraid we'll lose control of the situation over something rather insignificant (to us, at least). Mostly, these dramas are resolved, rationality enters, and the energy of the fight or argument dissipates just as quickly as it started. However, sometimes a referee (myself or my husband) must enter the fray and inject some objectivity into the situation. When I say, "You must take responsibility for what you did", they really don't want to, most of the time. Why say sorry and admit you're wrong when it's far easier to point the finger and say it's someone else's fault?

The problem is, most of the world operates like this. Blaming others makes us feel better and releases the tension of emotions we don't want to feel, such as stress, guilt, fear, or shame. Therefore, human beings mostly sit in the victimhood stage. It's not often we hear two children consciously having a discussion around responsibility in the playground, let alone hear countries apologise for their part in war or unfairly designed economic trade agreements. It's far easier to say "*you* made *me* feel like this" than "I'm sorry, I take responsibility for what I did". But why? Why is it easier to blame and shame than to accept responsibility for our actions, deeds, and words?

Why Is Taking Responsibility Hard Work?

Taking responsibility feels weak. Period. Having to confess or acknowledge a mistake feels like a failure, as though we've given our power away. It feels as if you are staring down the barrel of a gun when you must put your hand up and say, "It was my fault", and admit defeat. To the identity-based part of your brain—the ego (your subconscious), as Sigmund Freud (the grandfather of modern psychology) called it—admitting weakness feels extremely threatening, and it will do anything to move you from this feeling of pain to feelings of control and pleasure once again. In this instance, it's easier to renounce responsibility and blame the other person. But allowing others to make you feel a certain way is a perfect example of giving your power away. With that very thought process, you have chosen to allow something external to determine how *you* feel. As Scott Stabile (self-help writer and speaker) says: "Making someone responsible for your misery also makes them responsible for your happiness. Why give that power to anyone but yourself?"

You don't want to take responsibility because you decided a long time ago that life wasn't in your control. It happened to you, and you're a victim of circumstance. The subconscious is an extremely powerful yet unevolved part of your brain and is always considering the worst-case scenario, to keep you safe from danger. It's all about proving itself right, and weakness, "mistakes" or perceived failure feels uncomfortable and unsafe. These represent a real threat to your survival, so it's easier not to go there. Every fear you have of not being good enough or being rejected is going to come right up to the surface. Let's just blame others for what's happening, rather than take responsibility for our part or practice acceptance and forgiveness.

Once you take responsibility, not only do you lift the burden from others, but you take back control of your own life and your own decisions and how you want to feel. You start to become so powerful, you light up and become the person you want to be.

You're Getting in the Way of Yourself

"At the end of the day, you are the only one limiting your ability to dream or to actually execute on your dreams. Don't let yourself get in the way of that."

— Falon Fatemi

In the victimhood stage, we unknowingly attract, enable, and create situations, then blame others for it. My ex-husband was an alcoholic who physically abused me. I married him because I subconsciously feared being alone and didn't understand what love was, so I accepted that life to be the best it could be. The whole time I was in that relationship, I blamed him for everything: the drinking, the abuse, the stealing. But looking back, I realise there was only one person responsible, and that was me. This is what I thought I deserved. Ultimately only you are responsible for exactly where you are in your life right now, so you must stop apportioning blame to other people.

We enable and attract situations from our own place of lack and scarcity, but acknowledging and accepting this is the first step toward taking responsibility. Of course, there are many broken people out there that you might have attracted into your life (I did), but when you begin to realise and accept that your life is the outcome of the choices you've made, driven by the beliefs you hold and what you thought you "should do", or what you think is only available to you, then you can start to pour loving acceptance and forgiveness on yourself. There is no point in wallowing. The more you loathe yourself and condemn your actions, thoughts, and deeds, the worse you make your life and the more you stay stuck in victimhood.

When you take responsibility for what you've enabled because you didn't know any better, you can start to forgive yourself. This is you saying, "I'm doing the best I can. I'm doing the best I can." Take a breath, practice acceptance, and let go because resistance is pointless. Start taking back what is divinely yours—the power to create your best life!

Exercise

How responsible are you? Where in your life are you still justifying your actions? Where have you acted like the victim, blaming others for your misfortunes, but deep down feel bitter, resentful, and cross at life? Have you navigated your own life or are you where you are because of decisions, individuals, or situations you believe to be out of your control? Do you lack time, patience, being organised, money, commitment, love? What do you believe isn't or not available to you in different parts of your life? Do you make excuses for why things didn't happen or why you did something a certain way? Making excuses is a form of self-sabotage and fuels your self-limiting beliefs so you don't get what you want. When you make excuses, it's because you haven't learnt the lesson or aren't willing to learn from them. For example: "I have less money than I should because my rent is too high or my job doesn't pay me enough money. I'm unlovable or ignored because my husband doesn't listen to me. I'm not healthy because I've never been told what is best to eat."

When you take responsibility for something, does it feel good to know it was your doing, or does it feel uncomfortable and weak? A major part of taking responsibility is to accept all your emotions around the situation. Don't ignore or push them down. Process them and be honest with how you are feeling. Listen to your inner self—that voice is continually telling you how you are feeling. What is coming up? Feelings of inadequacy, failure, rejection?

Shining a Light on Responsibility

A good exercise to start challenging your lack of responsibility is to write a list of all those people you feel have wronged you in some way.

- How did you give your power away?
- How did you let others determine your outlook on life? (We feel attacked when others are rude or judge us, but first what they think is none of your business and if you feel triggered, this says more about your lack of self-worth and self-esteem.)
- How does blaming them help you?
- What are the hidden benefits of blaming them?
- How would it feel to take responsibility for situations you previously blamed others for? Does it make you contract and feel uncomfortable, or would you feel freer and more liberated from it all?
- Does it feel safe to take responsibility?

Know, in your heart, that when you take responsibility for all your actions, thoughts, and deeds, you *can* live the life of your dreams. Don't ruminate and dwell on things, be curious, question and challenge your thoughts. Stop complaining and start practising gratitude for what you are now aware of. Say thank you for all that is going well in your life, as well as your perceived mistakes and failures, as these were just lessons to take you back to your path of truth. Taking responsibility gives your life integrity, meaning, and credibility.

"When you walk with the trash, you start smelling the same."

— Anthony Liccione

It is your responsibility to be discerning of what and who you let into your life. Choose people who inspire you as they encourage you to grow. If you are around negative people who complain or blame, you will do the same and you'll slip down into victimhood again. When you complain, you lack "the ability to respond" or accept the present moment. It is said that you are the average of the five people you spend the most time with, so choose those five carefully. Do they uplift and support you, or do they drain your energy and bring you down, blocking your way to greatness?

Making the Choice

Now you understand that you can be abundant all the time, but your mindset must be right. It means you're no longer playing the victim. This is you operating with the firm knowledge that the power to create rests within *your* hands. When you raise your awareness and live from consciousness, making decisions from that place, understanding how life really works, *then* you get to be a powerful co-creator of your dream life, along with the universe.

This means being a responder, being proactive, conscious, and intentional about your decision-making. When you move into that second stage of awakening, you become aware that you are in the driver's seat and can cherry-pick what you want from life. You break free of perception and self-limiting beliefs and start living authentically as you—as you were born to be. You control your environment, *not the other way round, as you once believed.*

3

You're Living Someone's Else's Life (And You Didn't Even Know It)

"The way life is designed, we are programmed, conditioned, educated out of our power, because we have been programmed, conditioned and educated to please others, to do what others say and to do what others are doing."

— Iyanla Vanzant

There you are, living your life on automatic. You're thinking, "This is it. This is who I am and what life is . . ." Or is it? You're reading this book, so you must know that mentality hasn't paved the way so far. So what steps do you need to take to find your true authentic self and allow you to live a sacred life full of freedom and flow?

When you let go of all those external factors that cause you to think, feel, and act certain ways, and you see what's underneath it all, then you'll start discovering your authenticity—the voice of your soul. This is pure awareness of self. As Meggan Watterson says, "Before you can hear, much less follow, the voice of your soul, you have to win back your body. You have to go on a pilgrimage beneath your skin".

You're beginning to acknowledge and accept complete responsibility for your own life and can sit in the realisation that you unknowingly created and enabled it *because you didn't know any different.*

Knowledge is power, bringing awareness, understanding, and ultimately wisdom, but this is all part of the journey. For you to transcend to a life of authenticity and love, you need to understand where it all started.

The Three Parts of Your Miraculous Brain

According to Freud, your brain has three levels of consciousness: the conscious, the subconscious (referred to as the preconscious at the time), and the unconscious. The conscious part of your brain is the seat of critical thinking, where all obvious and deliberate thought takes place. It's where you make decisions—consciously aware and focused—and get stuff done. It's logical, rational, and organised, where incoming data from the world around us is filtered and analysed so we can go about living our lives. This is where the drivers of motivation and willpower reside. The subconscious sits just beneath the surface of consciousness, storing thoughts we are unaware of that may be pulled into awareness at any time. It is the home of all long-term memory, experiences, emotions, behaviours, habits, beliefs, and creativity. The bottom level of consciousness is the unconscious, which we have no control over or conscious awareness of. Here lies a mixture of deeply embedded thoughts and experiences, control of the autonomic nervous system, control of the immune system, and basic survival instincts.

The 3 Parts of the Brain - Sigmund Freud

The Subconscious

Though you may think you are living your life with intention, consciously making decisions, this is unfortunately untrue. Your unevolved subconscious brain is extremely powerful, believed to drive at least ninety-five percent of the way you live your life. It has been programmed entirely by the outside world (the conscious brain only evolved as an adjunct to the subconscious many thousands of years later). Therefore, you live on automatic—you're unconscious or "asleep". The subconscious is the "central processing unit" or hard drive of your brain, a two-million-year-old device that hasn't evolved since prehistoric days. It runs on beliefs, emotions, and attitudes. It is completely irrational and works lightning fast because it uses your stored life experiences to help make decisions to protect you from any threat and keep you safe. Its *only* job is to keep you alive and protect you from any threat. *Herein lies the problem to your greatness.*

Understanding How the Subconscious Keeps You Safe

Your unevolved subconscious still thinks you're living in a cave, so *anything* it perceives to be stressful is considered a threat to your survival. It cannot differentiate between a predator, or you are feeling overwhelmed by normal day-to-day demands. When you are triggered (i.e., a negative emotional response to something we feel unable to cope with), a cascade of stress chemicals are released to help you manage the perceived threat. Hormones such as adrenaline and cortisol are released, and blood drains from your forebrain, blocking memory receptors, stopping you from responding rationally or feeling any form of control. Your digestive system shuts down, blood rushes to your extremities, your breathing speeds up, your pupils dilate, and your heartbeat increases—all to help your body survive the *perceived threat*. This is known as the "flight, fight, or freeze response".

Any stress will trigger the same fear response, whether it's big trauma such as divorce, death of a loved one, or abuse, or little traumas like hating a job, a dwindling bank account, annoying co-workers, an angry boss, or spousal arguments. Being aware of this is a giant leap forward on your path to discovering your authenticity, even if you're frustrated you let this get in the way for so long. Forgive yourself; you weren't to know. Your subconscious will do anything to protect you. Therefore, when you feel under threat, it will work as quickly as possible to move you from pain to pleasure. Although this might have been effective in prehistoric times, in modern life it has the capacity to keep you from achieving what you want. This keeps you in survival and fear mode (victimhood) instead of expansion and love.

Your Childhood and the Creation of Perception

"Whatever we plant in the subconscious mind and nourish with repetition and emotion will one day become a reality."

— Earl Nightingale

When you were a child, your subconscious was like an empty reservoir, just waiting to be filled up with ideas, thoughts, beliefs, attitudes, emotions, and feelings. These go on to function as a blueprint to help you figure out how to navigate the world and ultimately how best to stay alive. Everything you heard, saw, and experienced—the behaviour and words of the adults around you; collective societal beliefs, traditions, and cultures; the behaviours of siblings and peers—started to form a story of how you saw the world, so you could make sense of it.

According to the neuroscientist, Dr Bruce Lipton, our brains are in a hypnotic state up until the age of nine or ten, taking everything they hear and see as truth. As we hear these stories on repeat, our brains become programmed to operate a certain way as we start to create beliefs in all parts of our lives. This governs our behaviour and becomes imprinted on our subconscious, creating our unique mental lens—or *perception* of the world. These beliefs create a feeling of certainty, or "comfort zones", of how much we can have or what is available to us.

When that "reservoir" is full, often just before puberty hits, it's as if someone firmly snaps the lid shut across the subconscious. Nothing can get in or out. Welcome to your unique perception of life, programmed and coded from the environment around you.

Perception is all based on your own *personal* experience of life. If your parents said you should work harder at school, or you're not as clever as your sibling, or you should be like this friend or that person, this can create the belief that you're not intelligent, not good enough, or not lovable. This could impact your ability to succeed in a career or have meaningful relationships. If you heard stories about life being hard work or comments on how expensive things were, these looping thoughts could create negative attachments to work or money or both, ultimately impacting your wealth potential or career success. If your parents argued a lot when you were a child, you may think you don't deserve a peaceful and easy home life, causing you to unwittingly create drama and arguments with your spouse or children. If you felt ignored or unworthy as a child, this can create feelings of being undeserving or powerless, so you create a reality where you feel walked over and no one listens to you. It's familiar, it's safe, it's your emotional home.

This means that even if you consciously tell yourself what you want, but those beliefs and feelings exist subconsciously, it is not possible to create that reality you so desperately desire. Your subconscious will win. Every time.

"You see persons and things not as they are, but as you are."

—Anthony De Mello

You *believe* what you see through your own mental lens; *you only see what you want to see.* You might consciously think differently, but your subconscious is five hundred thousand times more powerful than your conscious and *always* wins. It can process twenty million bits of information per second compared to the conscious brain which can only process forty bits per second.[1]

According to Lipton, we are already programmed through ancestral coding, even before we are born. He demonstrated that in vitro, the foetus is already responding—i.e., coded—to the environment

1 Bruce Lipton, *The Biology of Belief*, March 2005

around it. Not only is nutrition passed to the baby via the placenta, but chemicals related to the mother's emotional responses to the environment are also passed on through the baby's blood. Therefore, that baby has *pre-knowledge* of the world, downloaded information it could never be aware of, contributing to how it experiences the world.

Each of us is only aware of what we believe and the *meaning* we attach to our individual experience. That means the way you think, your habits, your actions, and your behaviour are completely unconscious—just a broken record on repeat. When you live boxed into your comfort zones, driven by fear and trying to stay safe, you can never be genuinely happy. It feels like we are always running back to safety and survival instead of walking towards what we want: love, ease, joy, peace and—essentially—freedom.

Comfort Zones and "Set Points"

"Only those who risk going too far
can possibly find out how far one can go."

— T S Eliot

As your unique perception is created, you lose the ability to tap into the potential you were born with (i.e., your authentic self). Instead, you stay within the confines of what you believe to be safe. These comfort zones exist for everything—how much money you earn, your weight or health, amounts of happiness, confidence, time, patience you have, your ability to attract and keep a loving partner, how far academically you'll push yourself, how much effort you put into things, and more.

How Comfort Zones Work

The top level of your comfort zone includes the best life can be—or the most of anything you believe you can have or deserve. These comfort zones act like an inner thermostat according to Gay Hendricks.[2] When life is going well, or we earn more than we subconsciously believe we are worth, we start to feel uncomfortable. It's unfamiliar and therefore feels unsafe. Thus, the brain turns down the temperature and we unconsciously *self-sabotage*, to bring us back down back into our comfort zone where it feels safe again, even if you're frustrated and uncomfortable.

We think, "Oh well, I'll probably fail anyway", or "I'm not good enough/skilled enough", or "I'm too old or don't deserve success, I'll never find a partner". These thoughts take us back to the lack mentality we were programmed with, making us feel negative about ourselves and causing us to act in ways that confirm our beliefs and return to that familiar comfort zone. You procrastinate and make excuses, you break your diet, binge drink after a period of sobriety, spend more or cause arguments in your relationships. Although you might feel safe, you are still ultimately miserable and frustrated, stopping you from moving forward in life.

Of course, there is a bottom "set point" to your comfort zone too. This marks how difficult life must get before you take action to bring yourself back up to where you feel comfortable. For example, if you're in a relationship with someone who doesn't treat you with the love and respect you deserve, they have to cheat on you or abuse you before you finally leave. Or you stay in a job you hate until you get fired. This is the point where you say, "Okay, no more. I've stepped down the ladder enough." My bottom "set point" was when my first husband physically abused me. I felt my face scrape across the kitchen tiles, leaving a large scratch along my left cheek. I had stepped down the rungs enough and woke up the next day knowing that this was *not familiar* and that I deserved to not have abuse in my life. So, I left him.

---

2 Gay Hendricks, *The Big Leap*, April 2009

There tends to be a lot of uncertainty around "set points" (especially bottom ones). Ask yourself if you only act when things are super painful for you. If so, then you're running away from things out of fear, trying to avoid feeling a certain way. You're in survival mode instead of working towards a world full of abundance, love, and happiness. You're not even thinking about obliterating your upper "set points" to create a magical existence, you just care about feeling safe and familiar again.

Your Life Is a Tape Recorder Playing on Repeat

Because we unconsciously think the same thoughts and stay in familiar situations, penned in by our own self-limiting beliefs, *you will create a future that's the same as your past.* Whatever you believe, you will attract experiences to confirm this belief, and this is how you'll see the world. Your brain is just a tape recorder of what has already happened. As Dr Joe Dispenza (neuroscientist and author of *Breaking the Habit of Being Yourself*) says, "If you're not creating your future, it is possible you believe more in your past than your future."

"Research on memory shows that most of it isn't even true," he continues. "Human beings make stuff up, reliving the past and not believing the life they want is available, so you're just reconfirming and creating emotions, so you don't change. Although you may consciously think you want something—money, health, a relationship—most of us are so strictly programmed that not even the smallest, flickering spark of an empowering belief will enter our body or mind." Many of us don't want to create a future away from fear or self-limiting beliefs. It's safer to live in the past.

This means you can't live fully, experience joy, or feel whole and free. Unless you change this narrative by rising above your ego using conscious awareness, you will have no power to create the life you want or reach your highest potential. You'll dim the light inside of you that is desperate to shine like the brightest star you are.

Your subconscious isn't going away, so you must learn to live with it, reprogram it, and transcend it so you can consciously create the life you deserve.

> ***"Everything we hear is an opinion, not a fact. Everything we see is a perspective, not a truth."***
>
> ***— Marcus Aurelius***

Let's start discovering the beliefs that have created your unique perception of life and where they have held you back.

In your journal, write down at least five beliefs you have about the different life domains. For example, in the career domain, you may write: "I must work hard to be successful. I will only be rich if I get a good job. I'm not good enough to work for the top companies in my sector. I'll never reach the top." For your relationships, maybe your beliefs are: "I need someone to love me, validate me, look after me. I need someone to complete me. There are no available men, all the good ones are taken. I will be a bad person if I'm divorced."

Now ask yourself these questions for each belief:

- Was there a specific time when this belief was created? When did you decide it to be truth?
- How old does that voice speaking those beliefs think you are?
- Where did that belief come from in the first place? (Keep asking this one. Once you understand this, you start to challenge the negative looping of the story.)
- Were you indoctrinated into these beliefs by things you heard or saw, or did you choose them consciously?
- Why do you want to believe this?
- Do you have evidence to support your belief?

- How does this belief serve you?
- What would you rather believe? What would a new story be?
- How would it feel if you didn't have these beliefs and pushed yourself out of your comfort zone?
- Does it feel safe to believe a different story?

Your Personal Comfort Zones

Ask yourself in which areas of your life you're living out of certainty and safety. Maybe you're staying in a job you hate (but you need the money), you're committed to a relationship that you're unhappy in (but you're scared of being alone), or you want to try new things (but you're scared of failing). When you live in safety, you're running scared - living from fear, not love. Therefore, you feel stuck because you can't grow and expand from fear. It's as if your face is pressed against a glass wall; you can see everything you want, but you can't get to it. So you stay in your familiar place, frustrated and resentful, telling yourself that you're not worthy or deserving, believing that abundance isn't available to you.

Acceptance

This means you had no conscious control over the curation of positive, abundant stories. Our own caregivers were just victims of victims, programmed from lack and scarcity, so how could they possibly teach us any other way? They were just doing the best they could with the resources, knowledge, and experience they had from *their* unique perception of life. They also never felt good enough, lovable enough, or worthy enough. Now you can start to open yourself to awareness, acceptance, and ultimately forgiveness, to help you step closer to your beautiful truth. Take a deep breath and start forgiving yourself for the little control you had, and get excited that you are unearthing the power to break free of the confines by which you lived your life.

Energy and Thoughts

"Whenever human beings consciously change their thought vibrations they can change their life."

—Amit Ray

Human beings are not just physical. We are also emotional, spiritual, *and* energetic beings. When you break our physicality down to the smallest atom of the smallest molecule, we are just energy. Everything in the entire universe—living and non-living—is energy, including all thoughts and emotions. That automatic unconscious thinking, which you give little regard to, is the most creative of all energy, the beginning of everything. *Every physical thing in the world once started off as a thought.* As Buddha said, "What we think, we become." That is how powerful your thoughts are and why your life is the way you *think* it is. The word "emotion" means "energy in motion". It's just an energetic vibration in your body that creates a feeling and helps us understand why we sometimes feel full of energy and on a "high", and other times feel flat, with little or no energy at all.

These atoms are in a constant state of motion. This is the Law of Vibration, the second universal law. These atoms vibrate at a certain frequency (the speed or rate at which something moves). You can't touch or see the energy of someone or something, but we can feel, sense, experience, or react to it.

"Everything is energy and that's all there is to it. Match the frequency of the reality you want and you cannot help but get that reality. It can be no other way."

—Albert Einstein

The fourth law of the universe, the Law of Attraction, states that "like attracts like," so whatever frequency that energy is vibrating at *will* attract the same back. It is this exchange of vibration that creates our reality. This is the definitive reason you are the personal creator of your reality. Every moment, your environment is reacting to your thought frequencies and the energy you emit. Therefore, your external world is a *direct reflection* of your internal state. You are always creating your reality from your thoughts and feelings, whether they be from an expansive state or from outdated false beliefs and the past. Everything that you manifest in your life is there because it matches the *vibrational frequency from your thoughts and emotions*. What we send out will attract a vibrational match back.

The Vibrational Scale of Consciousness

When you are feeling fantastic, happy, at peace, or in a place of love, you're experiencing high vibrational feelings—you're buzzing. When you're feeling low, sad, fearful, angry, depressed, or guilty, those feelings vibrate at much lower frequencies. You can physically feel the difference in your body.

The Vibrational Scale of Consciousness was designed by psychiatrist Dr David Hawkins, using over thirty years of research and conducting over 250,000 calibrations to demonstrate that different levels of thought and feelings resonated at different frequency vibrations. These were measured in megahertz (MHz). The higher the frequency, the happier and more peaceful you feel. The lower the frequency, the more miserable and depleted you are.

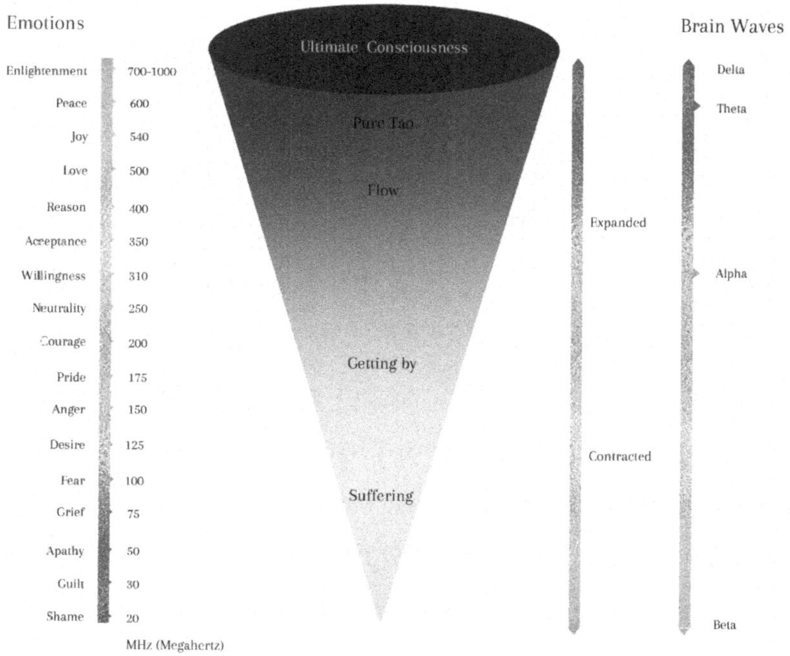

Vibrational Scale of Consciousness - Dr David. R. Hawkins MD. PhD

As humans, we have the innate power to create the highest vibrational energy we desire when we choose to live from a seat of consciousness, driven by how we feel about our beliefs and thought processes. In the first stage of spiritual awakening, we resonate mostly from fear and anger, so it is impossible to create the reality we want. If like attracts like, then isn't creating our ideal reality a simple case of adjusting our thoughts and making sure they are positive and happy?

How Do Our Thoughts Create Our Reality?

"Watch your thoughts, they become your words. Watch your words, they become your actions. Watch your actions, they become your habits. Watch your habits, this becomes your character. Watch your character, this becomes your destiny."

— Lao Tzu

Each time you think a certain thought, this creates a certain emotion and feeling in your body. When you feel an emotion, this feeds your thoughts, and on and on it goes. Your brain learns by repetition, so each time you think the same thing over and over, you are unknowingly conditioning your brain to believe this to be true. These repeated thoughts become deeply grooved neural pathways in your brain, which create this automatic and unconscious response. Sort of like a drop-down box in a software programme. Your brain listens to every single thought—negative or positive—and does not differentiate between reality and fantasy, taking all your thoughts literally. When you tell yourself things like "my kids make me crazy", "I'll never be loved", "my partner is difficult", or "I hate my work", your brain takes this to be truth.

The more you think these thoughts, the more they become your beliefs. It's self-perpetuating, like a movie on repeat in your head. *You think what you believe. You believe what you think.* This moulds your habits, attitudes, and behaviours, which ultimately become your reality. We are completely shaped by our thoughts.

Do you see how this determines the way you see the world? Do you think negatively and complain? You'll only attract negative situations. You think abundantly? You'll be blown away by the abundance that life wants to give you. Human beings think approximately six thousand thoughts a day so this has a massive influence on how you experience life.[3] If you want to find the secret to the universe, you *have to think* in terms of energy vibration frequency, and this starts with your thought patterns.

What do you say and think to yourself consciously and unconsciously that is creating these negative thought patterns? Do you say, "I can't afford that", "All men are untrustworthy", or "I never have enough time or money"? Keep asking with curiosity, not judgement. Take the opportunity at the end of the day to reflect where your thinking has been. Don't be angry or unforgiving of yourself here, just start taking an inventory of your mindset so you have the foundation from which to transform it.

Exercise: Thinking About Your Thoughts

- Do the thoughts you think serve you?
- Do you ruminate and sit in the problem, or do you sit in the solution?
- Do you spend time in a creative growth mindset, or do you feel stuck and frustrated?
- What have you created so far with your thinking, good or bad?

The Choice to Ascend to the High-Vibrational You

"It is only through your conscious mind that you can reach the subconscious. Your conscious mind is the porter at the door, the watchman at the gate. It is to the conscious mind that the subconscious looks for all its impressions."

— Robert Collier

---

3 Tseng, J., Poppenk, J. Brain meta-state transitions demarcate thoughts across task contexts exposing the mental noise of trait neuroticism. *Nat Commun* 11, 3480 (2020).

When we are in victimhood, we don't think we have a choice of how we think, but we actually do. You govern your thoughts. You are not your thoughts, *you are you*, and you are just *having* thoughts. Your greatest power over how you live is an awareness of choice, including the thoughts you have.

There is no need to live from fear or lack anymore. When you understand the power of your subconscious and why it works the way it does, you can hack your thought processes and override those beliefs to take you back to the blank, beautiful sheet you were designed to be born as. You can rewire your brain and obliterate those upper limits of your comfort zones. You just need to reverse engineer it by starting with your thoughts first. Changing your habits isn't the answer, you *must go back* to the underlying thoughts and beliefs.

I know you're super excited, and you should be! You get to upgrade your software to become the 2.0 version of you. When you focus on raising your consciousness, it's effortless. It happens in the moment and unfolds easily. Honour yourself and stop looking to the outside world for validation. Ask yourself if you want to live according to your fears, or to your truth and your dreams. Can you tell yourself a new story of just how incredible you really are?

4

Undoing What's Stopping You So You Can Be The Awesome Creator You Were Always Designed To Be

"The only person you decide to become is the person you decide to be."

— Ralph Waldo Emerson

Just like you learnt old beliefs, you can create new ones. You can download an upgrade from false outdated programming, so you have the power to create the reality you want and control your environment, not the other way round. It's time to transcend the victimhood attitude of the world and become the awesome creator you were always designed to be.

The secret to life is that you're meant to constantly expand, which is not possible when we experience life within self-imposed comfort zones. You only hold yourself back by unconsciously living in fear, reinforcing programming that isn't even yours. Now it is time to discover how to install that magical new motherboard in your brain so you can create the very best version of *you*. This is you, operating from that high vibrational energy of love, the same energy we are created from in the first place.

"Whatever your mind can conceive and believe; it can achieve."

— Napoleon Hill

You have the absolute power to control everything with your conscious mind, and therefore have the limitless capacity to change the meaning you give to life. You were not given the capacity to believe and conceive something without the ability to create it. Consciousness is the seat of creation, the source of who you are, so choose to use it with intention. You *can* transcend your subconscious and override those falsehoods that keep on recreating a life on repeat you don't feel in control of. The universe says yes to everything and wants to give you everything in abundance. It's all available to you, if you just believe it was possible. Joyfully embrace the knowledge that you have this incredible power to undo the blueprint you never asked for.

It's exciting and empowering to know that you have the power to return to your true self. This is what I am going to teach you in this chapter. You don't want to look back in anger or regret when you're too old to do anything about it. It is this which creates the massive disconnect and disharmony between your internal and external worlds.

It is too easy to wallow in victimhood, but it's time to pull yourself out of the trenches. By committing to this work, you'll understand why you had those experiences, what you are meant to *heal* from. This time, it's going to be different. It's going to be driven by your heart, your soul, your truth. Your subconscious isn't going to back down quietly, so here you will find several scientifically backed ways to undo these blocks that get in the way of your brilliance. Refuse to let the lens of how you see the world run the rest of your life, because it's completely incredible on the other side. Are you really going to let the seven-year-old version of you continue to run the show? Love your inner child and ask them what they need, so you can release them of the huge task of running your adult life and allow the grown-up version to lovingly take over the reins.

Giving Yourself Permission to Make the Choice

Real life will always happen. Curveballs will always be thrown at you. That is all part of the human experience. But ultimately, *we choose* what to focus on and the meaning we give to it. That single force controlling the quality of your life is *choice.* Knowing why you made the decisions you did is a huge awakening. Choose to create your very best life while you still have the wherewithal to do it. I guarantee that living according to your ego will never make you happy, but stuck in a place where those feelings of freedom or joy are just out of reach. You will always be chasing the next thing instead of *choosing to feel it right now.*

Choose to focus and commit to peeling back the layers, even when you feel vulnerable, because this process will bring happiness and fulfilment. Any deliberate change will feel potentially dangerous to your brain. This is a perfectly natural response. This is why a change of habit without a change in mindset rarely works, so you remain disappointed and deluded that you cannot have what you want. To change on a cellular level, we must adjust the beliefs and emotions surrounding why we don't have what we want. You are safe, whole, and loved, and you *will* come out the other side a shinier, happier, and more fulfilled version of yourself.

"We are what we repeatedly do."

—Aristotle

Self-Awareness

Self-awareness is seventy-five percent of eliminating your programming. You are already far more aware than you were when you started reading this book, just by understanding your beliefs and challenging them. As you discover how to leverage your conscious mind, you might ask why you have allowed yourself beliefs that aren't true. When you are aware of what you think, do, and say, you become conscious and mindful in your actions. You're aware of the automatic vortex of fear you have the potential to slip down. You'll check in with yourself energetically if it feels right to you by listening within and feeling your energy in everything you do. As you become more conscious of your *default* thinking pattern, you'll be more aware of where your energy goes. You'll know what brings up your greatest fears, which shows the emotional wounds that need to heal. You'll seek to send it in the direction of love and truth because you'll feel it in your physical body and know which feelings align with your soul's desires. Awareness is the seat of ascension, of growth, of conscious thinking, of expansiveness and listening within. It is *this* we need to use to live in an awakened and empowered capacity.

Triggers

Triggers are anything we experience that elicits an emotional response in the body. For the sake of this book, we are focusing on triggers that elicit negative emotions and feelings of contraction. Modern-day triggers might be from comments, judgements, situations, or the behaviour of others. When we are triggered, our brain seeks to move us quickly from pain to pleasure. We might subconsciously self-soothe by engaging in behaviour that brings short-term relief. Examples might be eating more (of the wrong foods), getting angry or irrational, shouting, shutting down, drinking alcohol, exercising too much, or tidying the house. Although it might feel good in the moment, releasing the energy of fear you feel, all this does is compound those underlying beliefs of unworthiness and unprocessed emotions because it keeps you in that fear loop of not being good enough or capable enough to deal with it.

Anytime you are triggered, practice self-awareness instead. In that split second before you slip into automatic thinking and go down the stress vortex, stop! Author and motivational speaker Mel Robbins suggests quickly counting down from five to break the initial response. Pour in loving awareness so you can step out and become the observer of the situation instead of being the unconscious reactor. Take a few deep breaths, in through the nose and out through the mouth, which will break the circuitry in your programming just by consciously recognising you are being triggered. Ask yourself some questions: "Why am I being triggered? What does this mean to me? Where does this take me back to? What fear is it bringing up? What am I feeling? Why does it matter so much to me? Am I seeing this situation objectively, or is it from perception? What is the belief surrounding this? Am I living consciously or am I experiencing emotions I don't want to have because of beliefs that aren't mine?" Your emotions will tell you everything you need to know because they are pure energy. You might feel fear in your gut (the solar plexus is a large energy centre), anxiety across your chest, or maybe your throat feels tight when you're scared or tense.

"Avoiding your triggers isn't healing. Healing happens when you're triggered and you're able to move through the pain, the pattern, and the story—and walk your way to a different ending."

— Vienna Pharaon

Triggers illuminate the emotional wounds you need to heal from—all the inadequacy you felt as a child. It's never about the actual situation, it's about the old, buried emotions that were never processed properly, revealing what still needs to be healed. Don't fear triggers; instead, be thankful for them showing you what you need to heal from and bask in knowing you are shining a light on it.

Those people in your life that irritate you the most? They are your greatest teachers. So welcome the triggers. The only way out is through, so choose to love yourself anyway as you stumble, learn, investigate, and pull yourself back up and out. When you are triggered, laugh at yourself, pour love on yourself for how you respond to situations. As you build awareness of your reactions, you build choice. As you build choice, you build deliberate intention for how you think, feel, and act, activating the prefrontal cortex in the brain, which is responsible for planning and rationality. Ask yourself what you would want to feel instead. How does feeling like this serve you? (Maybe it's been part of your identity for a long time.) What do you need to do to break state and remind yourself this is not you? It's extremely cathartic to give yourself permission to acknowledge what needs healing so you start living from a place of love, grace, and reverence for yourself. True healing takes place when you dare to go to those painful places and work from there.

By breaking state—stopping, recognising, and acknowledging—you gain the power to decide what you can do to bring yourself back to a place of love and truth. What's good for the body is good for the mind and soul, so when you feel yourself being triggered, do something: jump up and down, grab your headphones and listen to your favourite music, dance, run, journal, read, exercise—anything that feels good and stops that familiar fear reaction. This will increase your vibration and stop the unconscious response.

This is you using your conscious brain instead of relying on that old, faulty software. Then, in time, you'll notice fewer and fewer triggers, and the big stuff never comes. Use the world around you to challenge what thoughts and behaviours you participate in, and which are more authentically true to you. The universe will continue to give you situations that trigger you until you heal completely.

In this way, you can be more proactive and less reactive. Be open to receiving the feedback and practice forgiving yourself when you're not always moving forward. Be grateful for what is being shown to you and what still needs to heal. Remember: *you heal in layers.* This is all part of the process. Sometimes you will fail spectacularly and react in ways that defy your newfound self-awareness—we are just perfectly imperfect humans after all! Don't let this knock you off course. It is a *practice of self-awareness.* It is a new behaviour, so remind yourself why you are doing this and be conscious of your thoughts around it.

"By becoming self-aware, you gain ownership of reality; in becoming real, you become the master of both inner and outer life."

— Deepak Chopra

As you practice awareness, you start feeling brighter, happier, and more empowered. You operate at higher vibrational energy frequencies that refill your vitality and allow you to create the reality you want and be thankful for being shown what you don't. Your brain always seeks to provide you answers, so this awareness does it from your core authentic self. The more you listen to your heart and soul, the more you hack into the software. When you make decisions from that place, the brain suddenly starts thinking differently and installing the upgrade. Once you know something has shifted, you cannot unknow it.

Keep asking yourself, does it feel safe to choose what you want? If not, why? Remind yourself that *every time you live in fear, you're walking away from your best life.*

Challenging Your Beliefs

"Your beliefs, either positive or negative, helpful or hurtful largely determine everything you do and how you do it."

— Brian Tracy

Challenge yourself through awareness and question your beliefs. When you do, you'll see they are no longer true; they were just stories you told yourself. It's why you have to do the deep work to find who you really are underneath that self-imposed armour and programming. It's also a great place to start forgiving yourself and others for the way you've lived your life so far. You must remind yourself daily that allowing yourself to be happy *isn't* life-threatening.

Look back at the beliefs you wrote down in chapter 3. Write down the true cost of living with the negative beliefs you have been carrying around. Are these beliefs helping or hindering you? Fast-forward five years of holding on to those beliefs, and look back at your life. What did it stop you from going for? What did you miss out on? Do you procrastinate because you have a fear of failure?

Now think about the hidden benefits of having these beliefs. For example, you work in a job you don't really like, but your whole family approves of what you do. Maybe you married someone you don't really love, and you feel unfulfilled, but at least you're not on your own. Maybe you avoid trying new things because you're scared of looking weak or incompetent, but at least you don't have to worry about failing, feeling uncomfortable, or feeling out of control. These beliefs create safety and familiarity, so the short-term benefit is that you've moved away from fear (pain) but ultimately you stay stuck in a place you don't belong and can never walk towards what you want.

What if you didn't have these beliefs? What would you go for instead? How does this make you feel? Excited and positive? Confident? Motivated? What new beliefs do you want to have? Do they feel right? If you were to have the beliefs you really want, what actions would you be doing to show this? If a previous belief was that making money is hard work or that you'll never have enough, the belief might be that life is a struggle. So, what is the new story? Money flows easily, there's always enough money—start saying *this* to yourself. What actions could you be doing? Telling yourself there is always enough, managing your money more effectively, feeling grateful for the money you do have?

Now, for a few minutes, close your eyes and allow yourself to sit silently in the infinite possibility of how the upgraded, conscious version of you would handle all those areas of your life without these self-limiting beliefs. What does that look like? Feel like? Use all your senses as you allow yourself to bask in this incredible space. Recognise any resistance you might feel at the cognitive dissonance between the conscious and subconscious.

Living Consciously and Being Present

"We cannot create a new future by holding onto the emotions of the past."

— Dr Joe Dispenza

You *have* to live in the present. Take a breath to remind yourself to stay present and take in the miracle that is life. Spend time in meditation, which slows down the brain waves so you can be more self-aware. Where energy goes, energy flows, so choose to focus on what's really happening right now. Choose to stay present versus living in the past or future, as you cannot control either. You've been operating from the past, using your programming as a frame of reference instead of being present and conscious, making decisions from what feels true to you. Do you sound just like your mom? Do you react like your dad? When you live like this, you draw energy from the past into your present experience. Each time you judge yourself for past decisions, you do the same. When you live in a place of anxiety or fear about the future, your brain can't differentiate between reality and fantasy, so it thinks it is actually happening and creates an emotional response. *Neither* are conscious and both stop you being present, or consciously aware.

Rewiring Your Brain

"You need to pay attention to the situation, the new behavior, or the memory that you want to repeat or remember."

—John B Arden

To firmly cement new, empowering beliefs, you must "rewire" your brain. If you keep revisiting familiar automatic thoughts and feelings, you will keep recreating the same reality based on your emotions and past beliefs. You have to deliberately change the way you think and feel each day. If you let external experiences affect your inner state, *you need to consider how mindful and respectful you are of your truth, or if you are accepting of feeling powerlessness or unworthiness.* Choose to live in that beautiful state of consciousness and awareness, instead of the one based on falsehoods. When you realise you can change your thoughts and beliefs on a cellular level, you can get anything you want!

Neuroplasticity

For many decades, it was believed that the brain was static. As Spanish neuroscientist Santiago Ramon y Cajal stated, "In adult centres, the nerve paths are something fixed, ended, immutable. Everything may die, nothing may be regenerated." The brain was not considered to be a renewable organ. However, research conducted as far back as the 1920s shows that the brain *can* rewire itself over and over to believe something new. Karl Lashley demonstrated in 1923 that the brains of rhesus monkeys could be rewired.[4] This research continued throughout the 20th century to demonstrate that the brain *does* have the capacity to continually rewire itself to believe something new.

4 Lashley, K. S. (1923). The behavioristic interpretation of consciousness. I. *Psychological Review, 30*(4), 237–272. https://doi.org/10.1037/h0073839

This is exactly how we learnt as children, and how new habits are formed. This is the study of neuroplasticity. From when the brain develops in utero until the day we die, connections amongst neurons (brain cells) continually reorganise as we gather information and adapt to the world around us. Our brains are doing all of this automatically, constantly pruning connections and making new ones, all without conscious awareness.

These connections are strengthened in response to our thoughts, beliefs, and experiences. "Cells that fire together, wire together", creating those deeply grooved neural pathways leading us to live life on "automatic". In order to reprogram your brain, you need to hit Ctrl+Alt+Delete. You need to tell your brain a new story until *that* becomes the new belief. The more you tell your brain new stories, the more you strengthen the connections between the brain cells, and *this* becomes the new neural pathway and the new belief. The brain always wants to prove itself right, so you start acting in ways that are consistent with how you think and believe. Be intentional and focus on those new beliefs you want to create. Make your thoughts extraordinary, and your life will change. Your brain cannot tell the difference between reality and fantasy so tell it amazing things! *Make the unfamiliar, familiar.*

Catch yourself when you have thoughts that aren't true. Keep reaffirming your new beliefs and looking for evidence to support them. In just a few days, that new belief becomes "a knowing", something that feels powerful and true to you. It's all about paying attention and repeating it so those new connections become the new pathways of your thinking.

Breaking Out of the Comfort Zone

"The moment you change your perception is the moment you change your life."

— Bruce Lipton

When you challenge your thinking and beliefs, you start to create a massive perception shift regarding what you are worthy of. This can be extremely uncomfortable as you feel the dissonance between the conscious and subconscious, and is often why personal development is not a fun process! You're consciously making new choices, saying no to things you previously said yes to. Not only that, but those around you might challenge this "new you". You're putting boundaries in place; you're stripping off that old persona, and it isn't familiar to you or those around you. Why are you no longer accepting being spoken to or being treated like this? What are you doing that they aren't? You might experience more judgement and criticism from people wondering who on Earth this new version of you is, possibly losing some of them along the way as you calibrate up to your truth.

Remind yourself that as you progress on your path to greatness, any negative reactions from others come from their own fears, deficiencies, and inadequacies. It takes bravery and determination to keep from calibrating down to others' beliefs about who you should be. Have absolute faith that you are going to push through this dissonance and live according to who you truly are. This isn't your ego talking, this is you standing firm, believing in yourself, listening to what energetically feels right for you, and operating from a place of love and truth.

When you practice self-awareness, you deliberately break out of your comfort zone set points. You no longer accept certain things that you welcomed in the past. Decide right now how much you can push yourself to raise these levels, those non-negotiables that will make your life so much happier. Your minimum set point should be extremely high, and your maximum . . . well, it should be so high that you shouldn't even have one in any area of your life. Just keep telling your brain that this is who you are now and what you expect. The more you do this, the more you will create what you want.

Hypnosis

Hypnosis is an extremely powerful method to rewire the mind, breaking down and removing self-limiting beliefs, removing emotional barriers, and clearing them so you live from a place of authenticity. You can choose to see a registered hypnotherapist or try self-hypnosis—there are hundreds of hypnosis videos online. Do not fear them—it's not hypnosis like you see on entertainment shows. This is a process of tapping into your subconscious to shift your belief system. Doing hypnosis for at least twenty-one days can help to undo and shift those beliefs and implement new ones. I *always* go back to hypnosis when I feel triggered and realise I still have self-limiting beliefs to clear and wounds to heal.

Positive and Negative Thinking

The more you complain, the more your brain will look for things to complain about and seek evidence to support its beliefs. You need to reverse engineer how you think about things, including why and where it comes from. Remind yourself how good it feels when you're inching towards your best life versus the one on repeat and from lack.

Remember, your brain will do what you tell it to do. If you tell it positive, motivational thoughts, your life *will* become more positive and expand in those areas you put energy towards. Take responsibility, practise forgiveness, and set yourself free. It's your responsibility to look after the present and your future. Recognise and allow yourself to feel the discomfort of being triggered; it's a gift to you because you have something to work from.

Exercise

Just before bed, spend some time reflecting on your day and the things you did, said, and thought. How many of these were from a positive or a growth mindset, and how many were from negative, unconscious thinking? Don't be hard on yourself; you're just illuminating it all. Forgive yourself; most of the world thinks this way. Now you know there is a different way. What emotions are coming up for you as you think about your thoughts? Anxiety? Sadness? Guilt? Anger? What can you do to slowly shift your focus to more positive, empowering thoughts? Can you put reminders on your phone, listen to meditations on positivity, or place notes around your house so you see them?

Positive Affirmations

Repeatedly listening to positive affirmations can cement the wiring of these new connections and the neural pathways they become. It's all about paying attention and repeating the new beliefs you want to have. Science shows your brain will change. Create positive affirmations for what you want, such as "I easily attract success", "I am lovable", "I am deserving", "I am worthy of having the best life", "I am enough", or "It is safe to discover my truth". Keep repeating them until they become true to you. Say, "This is my new reaction when X happens".

You can make and record your own positive affirmations or listen to hundreds of recorded ones online. You can also write them down and read them diligently every day until they become the new soundtrack in your head. As you do this, close your eyes, cross your arms, and hold your hands together. Like a pretzel, twist your hands up and hold them together at your chest. Take a deep breath and really feel these new beliefs as if they are real. Crossing over your body means the left and right parts of the brain *have* to talk to each other, webbed together like a powerful information superhighway, which helps to install the new belief. This is you telling your brain a new story. *This is you thinking and speaking into being.*

It is said that it takes twenty-one days to form a habit, although I believe that to be a little short. According to research, it takes an average of about sixty-six days to reprogram your brain, so commit to reprogramming your beliefs for two months[5]. Even if it's saying new beliefs/affirmations in a mirror each day.

Emotional Freedom Technique

Whilst hypnosis, positive thinking, meditations, self-awareness, and affirmations help to rewire the brain effectively, you need to shift the unprocessed emotional component that stems from your old belief system. Otherwise, you are just papering over the cracks. You can keep thinking new, positive thoughts, but if you still *feel* a certain way, you will never truly believe it.

Understanding and facing your emotions head-on is the key to an authentic, epic life, so don't ever ignore them. The more you stick on that happy face, doing all the positive things you've been told and ignoring what you're really feeling, the more you ignore your true self. This is toxic positivity. You feel it in your energy, and it creates that disconnect between how you feel inside to what you experience outside. We are born with a whole spectrum of emotions, and it is only that we have been conditioned by well-meaning parents and caregivers to "let it go", "take a breath", ignore it and push away those darker more socially unacceptable emotions (e.g., anger, jealousy, hatred, and sadness). We've been taught we should be happy and positive all the time, but *this is precisely why you're not.* Those

5 Lally, Phillippa et al. "How are habits formed: Modelling habit formation in the real world." *European Journal of Social Psychology* 40 (2010): 998-1009.

darker emotions simmer just under the surface creating misery and discontent. To transcend your self-limiting beliefs, part of the work is allowing these emotions to be heard and be processed. You *must* fully experience the emotions you don't want to feel, then process and release them. When you've pushed these emotions down, this is what you resonate at, stopping you from getting what you want.

Emotional freedom technique (EFT) is a relatively new neuro-technology that helps to get rid of unprocessed emotions, negative thinking, and self-limiting beliefs. Used correctly, it has the power to massively transform your life. Originally developed by Gary Craig in 1995, it has its foundations in acupuncture, tapping on the same specific points of the body's energetic systems, sending vibrations through different energy meridians to disrupt any dwelling negative energy stuck there. EFT works by helping to neutralise those feelings by calming down the brain. I am an avid supporter of EFT, and the method in which I am qualified, the rapid relief technique (RRT), allows the energy from these darker emotions to not only be neutralised but fully processed and released so you quickly revert back to that vibration of love—the one you were designed to live from.

Journaling

Writing out your feelings without judgment helps you understand why you feel the way you do. Dare to explore some of your deepest yearnings and fears by writing down the truth. Getting those thoughts out of your head and onto paper transfers the energy. You can even go as far as safely burning the writing later to help shift the energy. Unconscious writing is a process from *The Writer's Way* where you write for approximately twenty minutes as soon as you wake up when your brain is still in the theta state—the fascinating border between the conscious and subconscious. It's a cleansing exercise to download all that is bubbling up in the subconscious, brought to the fore during sleep.

Meditation

Whilst in the theta state, the mind is able to achieve deep and profound learning, healing, and growth, which is why meditation is so powerfully healing to our mind, body, and soul. Meditation gives you focus and creates a peaceful, loving high-vibe state. As a result, you start to walk towards what you want because it allows you to quiet the noise and listen to your soul. This results in purer frequencies because they are from your truth. Start with short, guided meditations if you are new to this practice. Choose to do meditations on undoing self-limiting beliefs, accepting what is, letting go of negative thoughts, and forgiving self and others.

5

Self-Love

"The most important relationship in life is the relationship you have with yourself. Because no matter what happens, you will always be with yourself."

— Diane Von Fustenberg

What Is Loving the Self?

There is a lot of confusion around self-love. Many think it's egotistical, arrogant, selfish, or even a bit weak. We might think, "Wow! they love themselves way too much" or "She's so in love with herself". A person may seem to be doing what they want without a care or thought for anyone else. But this is what society mistakes for "self-love", and why we judge it so much. This isn't self-love. This is looking for validation, and it is driven by ego and fear. It's the act of seeking approval from the outside because of unmet emotional needs.

Self-love is you really loving your being and connecting with your soul as opposed to massaging your ego. It's having a deep sense of respect, feeling you deserve anything you want, and valuing yourself and your needs. It requires such kindness and compassion that you physically vibrate from a place of love. Love is one of the highest vibrational frequencies there is, up with peace, joy, and enlightenment. It is the frequency we came into the world with and are designed to *naturally vibrate at*. It is what the universe, source, or God is, and what already exists within us.

Understanding this means we can remain more in this higher frequency, even when faced with challenges. When you truly love and accept yourself, you're filling your love tank so full you create a reality where you and everyone in your world bask in your golden pool of love and light. You won't create the reality you desire, those feelings of freedom unless you start by truly loving yourself.

When We Don't Practice Self-love

When you ignore your needs, you're eventually going to become depleted, miserable, and resentful—operating from an energy of obligation. It's not uncommon (especially for women) that their dreams, goals, and desires are put on the backburner whilst they give everything they have to love and nurture their family. When this is done from a place of love, then happiness prevails. But when you're not fulfilled, those emotions of sadness, anger, and even grief are never far away. Society teaches us that we must tend to everyone else's needs first, so we act like martyrs, but this just feeds into our anger and self-loathing. When we demand "me time" or do something for ourselves, we might feel guilty or judged. Often, we do it to escape, and our intentions are not from a place of love for ourselves.

"Self-care is giving the world the best of you, instead of what's left of you."

— Katie Reed

This means the gap between where you are and where you want to be becomes wider and feels even more unavailable to you. You distract yourself from what you're really feeling (empty and emotionally numb) and do anything you think will fill your cup: shopping, binge-watching television, scrolling through social media, socialising, getting your nails done whilst texting a friend, escaping to a spa, eating junk food, drinking, doing drugs, having an affair, spending money you don't have. You'll feel satiated, happy, and fulfilled for a time, but before you know it, those dark feelings start creeping in once again. It's just a distraction from what you don't want to feel, taking you another step further away from your true authentic self.

Self-love isn't something that comes naturally to most humans, unless you saw your caregivers intentionally loving and accepting themselves, practising forgiveness and compassion. We weren't taught the importance of this relationship, so we don't believe we should value or love ourselves enough to put ourselves first.

If you want to start living your life—one where you are thriving, not just surviving—you *must* fall in love with the one person that is always going to be there for you: yourself. When you love yourself, this transmits to others, creating better connections with everyone in your world.

What is self-love to you? Do you really love yourself? Do you deserve everything you want? Do you believe everything you want is available to you?

Why Don't We Love Ourselves?

You were born at the vibrational frequency of love, which ensured your needs were met. However, we learnt very early how to get the most love, approval, acceptance, and validation from our environments to ultimately ensure our survival. Although love should be unconditional, it became *conditional* instead.

Over time, if you were told you were "too much" or "too noisy" or be quiet when you were upset, misbehaving, irritating, or annoying, you became programmed to believe this part of you was not acceptable. You buried it because it didn't achieve the feelings of love, acceptance, and inclusion you wanted. When we live from fear of rejection, we vibrate from an energy of scarcity and lack, always seeking approval and validation instead of a frequency of love.

Self-Hate: The Only Route to Self-Love

"The real difficulty is to overcome how you think about yourself."

— Maya Angelou

Human beings are born with a full spectrum of emotions—an enormous range, from the high vibes of pure elation to the low vibes of guilt, shame, and powerlessness. We close off the darker emotions such as anger, jealously, disgust, fear or sadness as a misguided form of self-love. In doing so, we become different versions of ourselves—the ones we believe will get the most attention and love, not the authentic version, which stops us from loving the incredible creations we really are. Truly loving yourself is one of the hardest things to do because we have been so conditioned to be someone we're not.

We never end up fully living as who we truly are. We learnt that when we were ourselves, it wasn't safe—something bad would happen. So we harden and close down our hearts, feeding into the hatred of the person we actually are versus the one we present to the world. This armour prevents us from giving and receiving the love we so desperately want because we give off an energy that repels others.

The Inner Child and Worthiness of Love

Love then feels like hard work—something to be earned. You think you'll be loved if you're good, if you help look after everyone else, or if you do well at school. We bury the "unacceptable" parts of who we are, but this just stops us from loving ourselves fully. It's as if the younger version of you, your *inner child*, runs your life. That inner child becomes your biggest critic and provides a negative chatter inside your head, like a running commentary of negativity. This stops you from being amazing! You're letting the small version of you run the show, still looking for love, approval, and forgiveness. Therefore you sabotage yourself and blame others for where you are in life and why you feel the way you do. Until you forgive yourself and start loving and re-parenting that inner child, you will keep yourself in a world of unworthiness and block the abundance of the incredible reality that is available to you. It can feel unsafe to love the authentic person inside you, but this is the only route to joy, freedom, peace, and love. The only person that can meet your unmet needs is you.

When you heal your inner child, you create magic. You light up the room, you radiate confidence, and you magnetise amazing people and experiences into your life.

Self-Hate and the Shadow Self

"The shadow is a living part of the personality and wants to lie with it in some form. It cannot be argued out of existence or rationalised into harmlessness. The problem is exceedingly difficult because it not only challenges the whole man, but reminds him at the same time of his helplessness and ineffectuality."

— Carl Jung

You pushed away these darker feelings out of self-protection, making you more likeable and acceptable, but all this does is feed into your self-hate. Denying these parts of you results in deep-seated anger towards yourself. It's not always apparent but it's there, bubbling just beneath the surface—*like a shadow*. As Mark Twain said, "Everyone is like a moon and has a dark side which he never shows anyone." The problem is that *this part of you is real* and part of your authentic self. These shadows are predominantly formed in childhood but are also created from traumatic life events, such as bullying and abuse, or from collective societal or cultural beliefs. When we don't acknowledge our shadows, they cause us to punish the parts of ourselves that hurt us physically and mentally, because we wish they weren't there.

When we see our shadows in others, it triggers us because we hate that part of ourselves so much. We judge them because we've been told they are horrible and unacceptable. My own shadows would be anger, reactivity, crying, and an inability to cope. These were things that I was not allowed to show. Sulking or having a tantrum wasn't allowed, nor was jealousy or differences of opinion. When I got angry, I hated myself. When I saw neediness in others, it made me hate my own neediness. I despised reactive people; I thought they were weak. When I saw laziness in others, I hated the procrastination and apathy I saw in myself.

Forms of self-hate include criticising and judging ourselves, brushing away compliments, mistreating our bodies via food or exercise (too much or not enough), drinking heavily, doing drugs, smoking, procrastinating, people-pleasing, caring too much about what others think, being disorganised, chasing our tails, managing our money poorly, attracting relationships that don't serve us, not feeling deserving or worthy, or devaluing the contributions we make to our environments. When it's bad enough, it can also include physically hurting ourselves. Basically, we punish ourselves for not being good enough. The more self-hate we have, the further we remove ourselves from the possibility of unconditionally loving ourselves.

When you tell yourself you're not good enough, ask who's standard you're basing that on. It is all an illusion, created from someone else's perception and fears.

Anger and Guilt

Anger and guilt are often at the root of our self-hate. Much of the anger we have inside is from not being unconditionally loved in our childhoods. Small children get furious, release their anger, then move on—much to the surprise of their caregiver! This is how it should have been for us as children, but we were taught that anger was wrong, weak, socially unacceptable, or unsafe. This followed us into adulthood, where we swallow our angry feelings instead of expressing them like we should be able to. That anger never goes away, it's just been pushed deep inside.

Guilt is a learnt behavioural emotion that benefits no one and saps you of your energy. Babies don't have any guilt; they cry, then have their needs met. Their vulnerability is a powerful tool that provides them with love, acceptance, and approval. Guilt is the opposite of what you're trying to achieve—high vibrations of peace, love, and harmony.

Self-Hate Work

"Only when we are brave enough to explore the darkness will we discover the infinite power of our light."

— Brené Brown

When you start putting the intentional energy of relationships into one with yourself, this will reflect in all the relationships you have. You are the source of your own happiness and have the power of choice, creating a whole new you, with passion and faith and a deeper connection to yourself. Your route to self-love is to process and pour love on this self-hatred and to embrace all the parts of yourself that you denied while growing up.

It might feel uncomfortable going into your "inner darkness", but this is where the healing takes place. The only way forward is to acknowledge those darker parts that exist in every human and *bring them into the light*. They are part of you, so allow yourself to experience these emotions, sit in them, and remind yourself that you are complete, whole, and loved. They need to be heard and accepted. Learning to understand them, where they came from, and what they are trying to tell us is extremely healing. Do meditations on your shadows to really love this part of you. EFT is also especially transformative for shadow work.

Instead of denying your shadows, ask what the hidden benefits of not being fully you could be.

Be open to what triggers you, then enquire as to why it bothers you so much. What feelings are brought up in you? (if you struggle with defining different feelings, look up a Feeling Wheel online). Be respectful of your shadows. You've tolerated them for so long, now is the time to lovingly pour awareness and grace on them. You heal in layers, and just when you think something is cleared, more stuff will come up. I am completely accepting of my darker emotions, and I tend to them lovingly, grateful that the universe shows me the parts that still need to be healed. Use what triggers you as your friend, as a learning experience that will take you ever closer to your truth.

Processing Anger

Releasing the anger you feel is huge part of your healing journey. Look back at your childhood. Were your parents angry people?

Were you allowed to get angry as a child? How did you process it? Sulk? Comfort eat? Withdraw? Rebel? How do you process your anger now? Is it okay to be angry? If not, why? Is it safe to be angry? Do you judge and criticise others for their anger?

Releasing the Anger

Sara Longoria (energetics coach and creator of RRT) has created a fantastic exercise to release your anger. Start by writing a list of all the people you are angry with (dead or alive). Add everything that makes you angry (e.g., bad driving, rudeness, or lateness).

Now that you have your lists, write all the things you've wanted to say to this person or situation, even if it's abhorrent. These are your feelings, and they need to be heard because while they are in you, this energy stops you being your amazing self! Get loud! Get crazy! Scream, box, hit the bed, tap, throw pillows around, and say exactly what you are feeling so you can process and release the emotion fully. Otherwise, it will stay stuck in your body, where they stay repressed and bring your vibe down, stopping you from loving yourself and getting what you want.

It's good to get angry and release that energy, but do it in a safe, private space where you can let go. Let that anger have its say; it is such a release when it's gone. Revisit your list often to see if there's still anger to be released. Love yourself for the work you are doing. It can also help to journal your thoughts after an episode of getting angry, to see who or what you can forgive. This allows you to analyse the experience and pour understanding into what is behind it to help you release it. Kundalini Yoga is all about the energies in the body and can also help release anger. There are many Kundalini anger release meditations online to help you release that energy.

Releasing Guilt

Write down all the things you feel guilty about. Be honest here—this is a private workspace. Maybe you've done some terrible things that you would never utter out loud. Would you do them again? No, of course you wouldn't. Remind yourself of this so you can process and release it.

Here are some of mine: Leaving a previous partner who told me he would kill himself if I left him, spending time working on my business when I "should" have been with my children, spending money that I hadn't earned, and moving to a different part of the world to no longer be available to my parents.

How is holding on to the guilt helping you? How much do you believe you are allowed to have (of anything—love, money, success, happiness), just by being you? Is it okay to receive bountifully? Do you feel guilty when people give you things? If you don't believe you are deserving, ask where this is coming from. Where did these feelings of guilt or shame start? When you see that most of it wasn't even your own doing, and from stories you hear, you can start to unblock what it is you want.

Self-Acceptance

"Let go of who you think you are supposed to be and be who you are."

— Brené Brown

As you go through the process of uncovering your true and best self, you'll find the person you're most angry with is often yourself. We blame ourselves for not knowing better, not making better decisions, or having the knowledge to deal with situations in a more consciously aware way.

When you decide to stop punishing yourself, process your self-hate, and acknowledge your shadows, you will start to feel a shift towards self-acceptance and inner peace. This opens the way to developing radical self-love. You won't care if you are getting external approval or love, it will start to shine through from the inside. Only you can allow this magic to shine through and you'll see how miraculous your life is.

You no longer allow criticism of yourself or others as you realise that others' disapproval is about their own self-judgement and perception, and in that, you can find forgiveness. When you accept yourself as is and truly love yourself, there is no space for self-hate. When you direct your focus of love and relationships into one with yourself, you become unstoppable and start to vibrate at a higher level that creates the incredible reality you seek. Love isn't conditional. It doesn't need to be earned, paid for, or chased after. It is available in abundance, but it all starts with you.

Cultivating Self-Love

"You, yourself, as much as anyone in
the entire universe deserve your love and attention."

— Buddha

Self-love is you choosing a life that feels good, over one that looks good. It allows you to bring yourself back to that high frequency you desire. It's you being you, living your truth. When you feel self-love and gratitude, it is the most amazing feeling. Life stays in a beautiful state, and nothing matters.

You can push yourself to consciously ascend so you don't feel the need to escape or spend years discussing with therapists, your friends or your spouse, ruminating and churning over why you're not happy. It might be finally accepting that nagging feeling (yes, your soul), telling you that this relationship isn't right or you need to get a new job. It's about listening to your heart, not what you think you should do for the ultimate validation. It's all about listening from love, not fear.

Loving the self is being disciplined and intentional about what it is you want in your life and going after it, no matter what others think. It is no longer running away from your fears; it's you being steered by your soul. It's you being discerning, putting boundaries in place, saying no to things you didn't before, and saying yes to things you previously thought too hard or unavailable to you.

It's possibly the scariest thing to do as you show up and be your true self, putting your needs first, being who you are deep down so you're not continually exhausted from putting all these identities on so you feel accepted and included—but it is what will bring you pure joy.

"When you fall in love with who you are,
the world then falls in love with you."

— Marisa Peer

Instead of distracting yourself, re-parent that inner child so they know you love them unconditionally. Spend time with who they are and assure them that they were only doing their best. Stop judging yourself and others. The more you judge yourself, the worse it will be. Instead, praise your inner child, love her, and nurture her. Tell yourself all those things you wished you'd heard as a child: "I love you", "you're incredible". Start saying these things to yourself every day. Ask what your inner child needs right now? A hug? Some time on her own?

"When you recover or discover something
that nourishes your soul and brings joy, care
enough about yourself to make room for it in your life."

—Jean Shinola Bolen

You must meet your needs every day—listen to yourself, love yourself, do good things for yourself. Listen to yourself energetically for every decision you make. Recognising your gifts and talents, trust yourself, and know it is safe to be who you really are and do what *you* love. You must love your authentic self as opposed to who you think you "should be".

Exercise

Write down all the things you love about yourself (e.g., how you're a good listener, how you'll go the extra mile for someone else, how artistic you are, how organised you are, how you make amazing birthday cakes, how you always lend an ear). Read this repeatedly to remind yourself just how wonderful you are.

Exercise

Spend time with yourself, in whatever capacity that is. Use your list of fifty things that make you happy to do something that fills your own love tank so you connect with yourself. Self-love needs to be meaningful, so it is unique to each person. Make sure this time is quality time or ask if you are distracting yourself from what you don't want to feel?

You deserve good things; it is *not* selfish and it *is* ok to receive this in abundance. If this doesn't feel right, ask why you are feeling resistance. What do you still need to heal from?

Pour Love on Yourself

Mirror Work

Mirror work has a huge capacity to help build love for yourself. Look at yourself in the mirror for a few minutes a day and say, "I love you", over and over. I found this extremely difficult in the beginning. I would look at my face and get angry at my regrets or poor decisions, or even just get mad at the new wrinkles that were slowly appearing. Now, I look in the mirror and say "I love you" or "you're amazing" every single day. And you know what? I really do love myself. Self-love is the ultimate fuel for living authentically, in alignment and abundance.

Positive Affirmations

Tell yourself affirmations around self-love every day. Say, "I am lovable. I deserve and am worthy of love. I have an abundance of love in my life. I always feel loved." Anyone can do it, you can too. Say, "I live in the overflow of love. I am being powerful. I am being me. I believe in myself. It is safe to be loved." Tell yourself, "When I make time for myself, life is wonderful." Keep saying this over and over. When you change your belief around this, you change the energy around it too.

6

The Art Of Practising Forgiveness

"The first step is to understand that forgiveness does not exonerate the perpetrator. Forgiveness frees the victim; it is the gift you give yourself."

— T D Jakes

What Is Forgiveness?

Forgiveness is often defined as a *conscious*, deliberate decision to release feelings of resentment toward others who have harmed you, regardless of whether they actually deserve your forgiveness.[6] Although we might believe that forgiveness is just towards others, it is also a deliberate practice we must do towards ourselves to truly become free.

Forgiveness opens your heart to start loving yourself and feeling that deep sense of connection with others we seek. We often have trouble forgiving in the victimhood stage because we want to make others responsible for our thoughts, feelings, and experiences. Forgiveness feels weak and hard at the same time. Our egos feel damaged from relinquishing people or situations that have wronged or hurt us. But ultimately, we let it in; we allowed this to happen. It feels safer not

---

6 http://www.greatergood.berkeley.edu

to forgive, as if staying angry protects us in some way. When we forgive, we think we are excusing it, which feels weak. This is entirely unconscious and *not taking responsibility*. When you are unwilling to forgive, it hurts you. That energy of anger accumulates in your body, holding you back from being the awesome and lovable individual you truly are. Forgiveness isn't about condoning or excusing others; it's about setting you free.

Each of us has different learned capacities of forgiveness taught to us by our caregivers, peers and elders. Some of us have been taught to "forgive and forget" or "move on", whereas some of us have been taught to hold onto a grudge or situation so you are "forewarned" and not "caught" next time. If your parents easily forgave each other or said "I'm sorry" to you for things that upset you, you might be quite good at forgiving—towards both others and yourself.

Forgiveness dissolves the fear generated from the ego, but you will only release the past that holds you back if you are willing to forgive. *The person you find hardest to forgive is the one you need to let go of the most.* This might be a bitter pill to swallow, but it's a sign of empowerment. You only had the life experience, beliefs, and resources you knew of to make decisions, so can you now also forgive yourself a little? It is so empowering to know this, and forgiveness comes so much easier. You must forgive the things you and others did. Humans make mistakes; these are lessons to learn from, and in that, you can find gratitude.

What did you learn about forgiveness as you were growing up? Were your caregivers forgiving of you, each other, other people, or themselves? Did forgiveness come easily or was it brushed under the table, causing feelings of unresolved resentment and anger? How do you operate now? Are you forgiving? Do you hold grudges? Does it feel safe to forgive?

My perception of forgiveness was that it was hard—that people should be held for ransom and feel the pain of their wrongdoings. As if they should apologise to me, and they deserved my anger for what they had done and *how they had made me feel.* Once they crossed me, a line would be drawn in the sand. I saw forgiveness as something weak, pardoning someone else's behaviour at my expense. Now I understand this was my ego talking. It felt safer to distrust others and hold friends at an arm's length, yet I found myself sad and wondering why I couldn't create the closeness and connection I so desperately craved in my relationships. Subconsciously, I never believed I was worthy of an easy, happy life with loving individuals. Little did I know that in creating those walls; I imprisoned myself emotionally and energetically.

It is simply not possible to feel the vibrations of pure love when we live with unforgiveness. It is liberating to know you might never get an apology for the things that hurt you. Why? Because most of the time, people have no idea what they did or said had such an impact on you (and if they did, this is all because of their own emotional wounds). *You* were the one that gave meaning to it, not them. Humans are egotistical—they are too caught up in their own issues. *Hurt people hurt people*, as the old saying goes, because it's the easiest way of releasing their pain—and the world is full of them. Emotions are just energy, and when there's too much or you don't have conscious awareness over your emotional response, you're going to react and potentially explode, like a pressure cooker. If you don't have the right outlet, this can lead to some of the "unforgivable acts" we see in the world today. I put quotes around that word because *everything* is forgivable, even the worst things. That might be hard to accept, and many things that happen are not okay, but when you understand that the person was only operating with the tools and knowledge they were programmed with, it paves the way to forgiveness.

If you continue to not forgive people or situations, you will collect a huge pile of miserable memories over the course of your life that keep you in a state of blame, resentment, and victimhood.

Why Forgive?

"To forgive is to set a prisoner free
and discover that prisoner was you."

— Lewis B Smedes

If you want to level up from victimhood to empowerment, you *have* to forgive. The person that wronged you has no idea that you're that angry, twisting yourself out of shape whilst you ruminate over the situation keeping you stuck energetically, ruminating and unhappy. If you truly want to be free, naturally happy with your most authentic self, and living to your highest potential, all from a place of love, forgiveness is key.

Research conducted by associate professor and psychologist Loren Toussaint shows that forgiveness overall equals more happiness and better health, both physically and mentally.[7] People who forgive are less likely to be depressed and anxious and more likely to be happy. That's quite motivational, don't you agree? Even if it feels hard at first, being *willing* to forgive is the start.

"Forgiveness does not change
the past, but it does enlarge the future."

— Paul Lewis Boese

When we forgive, it allows us to let go of negative emotions that cause us to respond in unconscious ways. This lets you continue to

---

7 Toussaint, Loren. "Forgiveness, Stress, and Health: a 5-Week Dynamic Parallel Process Study." Luther College. 2016. https://pubmed.ncbi.nlm.nih.gov/27068160/

evolve and live in an expanded capacity, no longer tarnished by your misgivings of others. When you truly forgive someone, you stop pointing the finger, judging, and criticising that person. You accept that their experience of life is different from yours. It helps you see the pain of others from a place of empathy, support, and love. They are just human too; they make mistakes now and again. It's not wrong or right, it just is. After all, we are one collective energy, and the reason we feel things so deeply is because of these energetic ties we have to each other. Ultimately, we are all just doing the best we can with the knowledge we have. Forgiveness contributes to the greater good, the increased consciousness and love frequency of the world, so anger doesn't dominate. You rise above the pain, valuing and respecting yourself because you know that holding on to the anger will block your path to brilliance.

"Forgiveness is a process of giving up the old for something new. Old experiences and memories that we hold on to in anger, resentment, shame, or guilt cloud our spirit mind. The truth is everything that has happened had to happen. It was a growth experience. There was something you needed to know or learn. If you stay angry, hurt, afraid, ashamed, or guilty, you miss the lesson. You will be stuck in a cloud of pain."

— Iyanla Vanzant

Everyone is only operating in the capacity they know at different levels of understanding and awareness. By understanding that, we can forgive. Those who are mean have learned this as a way of coping, just as those who are full of hate or violent have as well. As adults, this is still within us. We are enraged but don't know a different way to release the pent-up tension. People that hurt others always have unmet emotional needs, which stem from their own pain. I'm not saying it's okay, but that it's good to understand, so we can process our feelings to reach a point of forgiveness.

Practising Forgiveness

Say you're fighting with your partner, and you think they should be apologising for something they did to upset you. Are you going to sit and stew in the situation, adding that misdemeanour to your ever-growing list of misgivings towards that person? Or can you process what's going really going on and why you feel triggered, to understand, forgive, and move on? Which one feels more empowering to you? It doesn't hurt or bother the other person if you're unwilling to forgive, but it does *ultimately hurt you*—physically, mentally, and energetically. Each time you recall that unforgivable situation, your brain relives it. This triggers the stress response, creating all those upset feelings, and your energy centres close down—especially those around your heart.

The alternative is to stop and work on forgiveness to release yourself. Your willingness to forgive is the first step, even if you don't know how. Whoever you need to forgive, accept that they are also suffering and are not consciously aware of why they behave the way they do. It is possible to reach a place where you are able to observe *why* that person acted the way they did, and even feel empathy for the situation. In time, instead of reacting to situations that once triggered you, you will look at them from a place of love and compassion.

Forgiving means you're freeing yourself, but as you do, take some time to sit in the anger and rage that comes up when you think of those people and situations. Journal, meditate, cry, tap, and voice it out loud. You need to process the emotions before you can move on, and these feelings want to be heard. Otherwise, the energy they emit will keep you in that place of frustration, anger, and resentment. Everything in the world is forgivable. Being unwilling to forgive is worse.

Exercise

Write a list of all the people that have wronged you throughout your entire life. Go all the way back to your early school days. Mine included kids in kindergarten, co-workers, teachers, ex-boyfriends, an ex-husband and old friends, right up to the present day.

What do you gain by not forgiving these people or situations? There are always hidden benefits. For example, perhaps you don't forgive your ex-partner for cheating on you, and therefore you are able to blame them completely for what happened. Who has the power over your feelings? Does it feel safe for you to forgive them? Do you think they might hurt you again or that you are condoning their actions? What would happen if you accepted what happened and forgave past wrongdoings?

Routes to Forgiveness

Mirror Work

Look yourself in the eye and say, "I am ready and willing to forgive [the name of a person who has wronged you]". Repeat this a few times. What emotions come up? Do you feel ready to forgive, or do you feel resistance? If you feel resistance, then ask:

How does it serve me not to forgive?

Does forgiving make me feel unsafe? If yes, why?

Am I being held back if I don't forgive?

What would happen if I let go and forgave the past/person?

Visualisation

Imagine forgiving someone who has upset you. Really sit in the memory of the situation and feel the emotions as if you were to let go. Say, "I forgive you", and release this person. Even though you might initially resist this process, doing it repeatedly can help shift the energy around it. Also, saying, "I am willing to forgive and open my heart to forgiveness", daily can help.

Negative Cord-Cutting

This is a process where you envisage diffusing the negative energy and *cutting the cord* which attached you to the person who wronged you. It is a highly effective tool if you do it repeatedly until you feel no more negativity towards that person. Again, this is freeing you of the negative energy around the situation. There are hundreds of specific meditations online you can do to help you navigate this.

The Nine Steps to Forgiveness

Dr Fred Luskin, director of the Stanford University Forgiveness Projects, is a pioneer in the science and practice of forgiveness. He developed the "Forgive for Good" method of forgiveness, which is a nine-step tool that has helped thousands of people across the world to forgive and release their grudges.[8]

How to Forgive Using The Nine Steps

1. Know exactly how you feel about what happened and be able to articulate what is unacceptable about the situation. Then talk to trusted individuals about your experience.
2. Make a commitment to feel happier about the situation. Remind yourself that forgiveness is for you and no one else.
3. Forgiveness doesn't necessarily have to mean reconciliation. Remember that forgiveness is to seek peace and understanding that comes from not blaming others.

---

8 Luskin, F . Forgive for Good: A Proven Prescription for Health and Happiness. New York, NY: HarperCollins; 2002.

Instead of reacting to those situations, you become an observer and responder.

4. Recognise that the primary distress is from hurt feelings, thoughts, and physical upset now, not what hurt you two minutes or ten years ago. Living in the energy of the past just brings up resentment of situations you cannot change. Remind your brain that it is not happening now, so you don't recreate those feelings on repeat.
5. When you feel upset, stop the fear response by practising self-awareness. What's really going on? What feelings are being triggered in you? Sit in it, process it, and challenge it. Is it real now? What would I rather feel?
6. Give up expecting things from other people in your life that they do not choose to give you. Recognise the "unenforceable rules" you place on their behaviour or your own. You can only control your own thoughts and actions, not others.
7. Instead of ruminating and dwelling on the past, focus your energy on creating positive experiences in your life now, rather than through an experience that has previously hurt you.
8. Instead of focusing on wounded feelings and giving power to those that hurt you, focus your energy on creating abundance in your life; look for love, beauty, and kindness around you. Forgiveness is about personal power. As Gandhi said, "It is an attribute of the strong."
9. Honour and respect yourself for forgiving. You are choosing to do this as part of your incredible growth. You have made the heroic choice to forgive.

Forgiveness is a process and can take time. Be compassionate and caring, respecting why the individual operated that way or why the situation happened. As soon as you can make yourself aware of this, it releases you from the shackles of resentment and anger. When you forgive, you also give yourself the powerful choice of how much you keep this person in your life. You make the decision of whether you keep them close or at arm's length, emotionally or physically!

Self-Forgiveness

"In order to heal, we must first forgive . . .
and sometimes the person we must forgive is ourselves."

— Mila Bron

Forgiving yourself is as important as forgiving others. A lack of self-forgiveness is caught up in self-hate, unworthiness, inadequacy, guilt, and shame, which stop you from living your life fully. These feelings resonate so low on the Vibrational Scale of Consciousness that you will create a reality to match those feelings. When we don't forgive ourselves, this keeps us miserable and living in fear. It doesn't serve you in any way. When you forgive yourself for past wrongdoings and realise you only operated from programming and coding that dimmed your light, you start to feel liberated. This increases the amount of love you give and receive because your energy frequency is higher, which ultimately impacts your entire life. The guilt, the shame, and the stories—they have to go! Say to yourself: "I support you and love you *no matter what.*"

When you forgive yourself for every mistake you've ever made, you'll become free of the need to sabotage yourself because you'll realise you were only acting in the confines of your own perspective, influenced by wounds that never healed. A huge part of forgiveness *has to be* towards ourselves in order for us to grow and become conscious. When we can forgive ourselves, we find it easier to forgive others. We often advise others to forgive themselves for past mistakes, but it's harder to point the finger at ourselves. What you say to yourself both inwardly and outwardly can reveal your level of self-forgiveness. Would you be as mean to a friend as you are to yourself?

When you do things that seem wrong or shameful, do you give yourself the forgiveness you deserve? Of course you don't. You walk around thinking what a terrible human being you are. You must be the worst person in the whole world, for whatever it was you thought, did, or said. You can't even possibly bear the idea of relinquishing fear and guilt; that would feel even worse! All this does is feed into your self-loathing, getting out a big stick to beat yourself up with. See how mean we are to ourselves?

Imagine you were chatting with someone who sat on the same park bench, and you realise it is the younger, less worldly version of you—your fifteen-year-old self. She looks at you, eyes welling up, and says, "I just can't hold it in any longer, I *have* to tell someone what I did." You hold her hand as she looks down in shame, feeling terrible guilt for the deed that happened.

She tells you the story, and you—the older, wiser, more experienced version of her—gently reassure her and say, "Oh, it's okay. You just made a mistake. We all do, It's all part of life."

You give her a big hug, let her cry and she says, "Thank you, you're right." She takes a deep breath, wipes away her tears and says, "Phew, I feel so much better."

Doesn't that feel good? So why can't you do this to your now-adult self?

If you lack feelings of forgiveness towards yourself, look yourself in the mirror and repeatedly say, "I'm sorry, [your name]." Looking into your eyes, say it slowly, deliberately, and sincerely. Maybe tears will flow as you slowly start to forgive yourself. Are you feeling resistance? If so, why? Do you think you don't deserve to be forgiven? Everyone makes mistakes (choices); that's part of life. And there is no such thing as failure. Failures are you learning to get back on your path again. You learn from these lessons, evolving and levelling up to your conscious awareness.

Forgiving the Inner Child

Self-forgiveness is all part of the practice of self-love and starts with forgiving your inner child—that little kid who just wanted unconditional love and didn't want to feel ignored, rejected, or disapproved of. The one that hid away the parts of you that didn't get unconditional love and approval, which just fed into your self-loathing. When you forgive the inner child, this is you saying to yourself, "It's okay. You're heard, you are enough." It's you saying to yourself, "I'm sorry I wasn't there for you. I'll love you; I'll parent you now. I'm there for you and I'm going to love you like no one else could ever love you."

Inner Child Visualisations and Meditations

One of my favourite techniques is to visualise holding the smaller childhood version of you. Sit quietly with your eyes closed and take a few deep breaths. Imagine you have your smaller self sitting on your lap. Ask them what they want to tell you. Let them be heard and let them feel your love as you hold your arms around them. Just let them cry, and stroke their hair. Remind your inner child that you will love them, that they are in an adult world now, and that you will always listen to them and give them what they need.

The 4Rs For Self Forgiveness

A beautiful logical process-driven method called "The 4Rs" can help you truly practice self-forgiveness for past actions or deeds.[9]

---

9 Cornish, Marilyn A., and Nathaniel G. Wade. "A therapeutic model of self-forgiveness with intervention strategies for counselors." *Journal of Counseling & Development* 93.1 (2015): 96-104.

Step 1—Responsibility

Accept and acknowledge your role in what happened and why it bothers you so much. Stop making excuses or pointing the finger at others. Take responsibility for what happened, accept what is, and show compassion and grace to yourself. Stop living in the past, feeling anger, resentment, guilt, or shame, recalling and judging yourself. The only reality now is the present, and you can't change the past.

Step 2—Remorse

When you take responsibility, you may feel remorse. This is good, as you can be thankful for knowing what you did or didn't do wasn't okay. This acts like the foundation for you to get past this. Although feeling guilty implies that you are indeed a "good" person, and you just behaved "badly", shame tells you that you are a bad person, which can make you feel very unworthy. Ask what's really going on here; are you really bad or was it just your behaviour? If it was your behaviour, this can be changed, because you acted unconsciously.

Step 3—Restoration

Taking action to move past your guilt or shame helps you amend your mistakes. Apologise if it is called for and ask what you can do for the person. Sit in meditation or journal to help you learn and grow from this. When you "fix" the mistake, you no longer wonder if you could have done more to amend it.

Step 4—Renewal

Everyone makes mistakes. This is a fact and part of the human experience. Everyone does things that they regret. Accept that you are not perfect. Focus on what you've learned, be thankful for what came up, and be willing to move past it and on with your life without dwelling on situations that cannot be changed.

7

Gratitude

"Gratitude is the healthiest of all human emotions. The more you express gratitude for what you have, the more likely you will have even more to express gratitude for."

— Zig Ziglar

Up until the COVID-19 pandemic and subsequent lockdown, the noise of the external world and juggling of normal family life had been too loud. But once again silence and stillness opened up, and I was given the gift of time as the volume of life was turned down a few decibels. It was a beautiful reset for my mind, an opening of consciousness to truly discover who I am and what I am meant for. I feel eternally blessed and thankful for the opportunity that came my way. I will always be grateful to the universe, who gently guided me and put people, books, courses, meditations, and time in my path so I could align with my truth and help you discover yours.

When I was a child, every December 26, I would sit down at our dining table and diligently write thank-you letters to grannies, aunties, uncles, and friends of my parents for the various gifts I had received for Christmas that year. I was not allowed to play with new toys or watch Christmas TV until what felt like endless thank-you notes were written. I treated the process as a chore and something to get out of the way as quickly as possible. So, over the years, I became quite skilled at speeding up the process. I would change the name at the top of each letter and the wording of the gift, but say the exact same thing in the main body of each letter: "Yes, thank you, we had a lovely Christmas", "I hope you did too", "I received X, Y, and Z", and so on until all the letters were finished and I was free to play with my shiny new toys.

I was conditioned to do this, so I never challenged it. Aside from the Christmas thank-you's, it was accepted practice to say thank you for meals cooked by my mother or birthday presents bought for me. Looking back, though I now know gratitude to be the most natural way of being, I highly suspect it was done from programming at the time. I knew in my heart it was the right thing, but I don't think I was *consciously or deeply thankful* or felt particularly blessed for all that was given to or done for me.

Although I might not have enjoyed the laborious process of writing the letters, it certainly created a foundation—a neural pattern in my brain—to say thank you. Think about it: how often do you just say thank you without truly feeling gratitude? Just done out of habit, formed by a belief it is the "right" thing to do?

A Key to Getting What You Want

"Gratitude turns what we have into enough."

— Melody Beattie

Gratitude is *another part* of creating what you desire in life, but staying in this high-vibrational place of gratitude often doesn't come easy for most. Why? Because most humans are angry, operating from victimhood, blaming and shaming everyone else for where they are in life. We take what we *do* have for granted, instead of feeling joyful for all that we have. We judge and complain, bringing more negative experiences into our lives, confirming our belief that nothing is ever enough, and *focusing on what we want more of than what we have.* We expect things, taking even our precious existence for granted. We give our power away to others and let them make us feel taken advantage of, and question why we should bother feeling thankful when others aren't in turn grateful for our efforts. Our egos feel bruised, so we slip back into feelings of unworthiness. Gratitude is seen as nonsensical, unnecessary, and is even perceived as weak by some. It might not even feel safe to be grateful or feel love at this level.

Having gratitude will unlock an easy, happier life. If you don't feel gratitude for things, you must investigate why. What is the blockage? Are there beliefs holding you back? Do you still need to work on forgiveness?

The Power of Gratitude

The significance of gratitude has woven its threads throughout time. It is repeatedly referred to in religious texts as the cornerstone of abundance and the key to creating a magical, meaningful life. As Rhonda Byrne (author and producer of *The Secret*) says, "Gratitude is what has been mystifying people for centuries." In biblical texts, it says, "Whoever has________ will be given more and he will have an abundance. Whoever does not have________, even for what he has, will be taken away from him," meaning whoever has gratitude will be given more and he will have abundance. Whoever does not have gratitude, even what he has will be taken away from him. (Matthew 13;12) *The missing piece of the puzzle is gratitude.*

"Acknowledging the good that is in your life is the foundation for all abundance. It's you deliberately and intentionally practising gratitude for what you have in your life."

— Eckhart Tolle

As I "unbecame" who I thought I was, I started to understand the magical mystery of gratitude. As I listened within, I started practising gratitude for everything and anything, and watched my life start to change for the happier. I had more energy, I brought joy to people's lives, and this was reflected back to me. Wow! These feelings of gratitude were amazing, powerful, and created those high vibrations of joy and love inside of me, versus waiting for others to make me feel this way.

Practising gratitude from a place of love and truth can *only* come from the heart, not the ego. I feel gratitude from an open-heart space, full of love and thankfulness for the blessed life I have. The type of gratitude I'm talking about is resonating from that deep, beautiful frequency of love. With sincerity in your heart, you no longer need to rely on the external world to create these feelings; you're operating from love, not programming and fear. I am thankful for *everything* in my life. I can find gratitude in the good things, the small things, the terrible things, the challenges, and everything in between. I know the power that practising gratitude has in my life. When truly felt, it has the magical ability to bring ease and happiness to your life in ways that you can never imagine. However, being grateful isn't automatic (although it should be) because the subconscious is a powerful piece of software programming, often negative dominant, so I have to catch myself if I'm saying things that satisfy my ego, not my soul. It takes time, patience, and practice, but with self-awareness, it is possible to stop your ego in its tracks. On the opposite side of the coin, if I am not thanked, I ask myself why I want to be so much. Why is feeling appreciated so important to me? Why does that trigger me? As soon as I challenge it, become curious, and remind myself it's conditioning, the fear dissolves. I remind myself I am loved and the need for external validation disappears.

The cultivation of gratitude paves the way to that destination of freedom and inner happiness, but it is an art, a practice, not just an attitude. To feel joy, you have to practice gratitude. As Brené Brown says, human beings are quite scared of joy. We are scared it will be taken away because we are designed to be on alert and on the lookout for danger. If we feel too much joy and rise above the upper limit of our comfort zones, we bring ourselves back down to the happy levels we decided we were allowed, not able to experience true peace or freedom.

Love and gratitude are *the* answer to a happy life. When you open yourself to gratitude, you open yourself to everything that is available to you. It has been scientifically proven that people who practice gratitude have better and more fulfilling relationships and connections, more patience, satisfaction, increased happiness and mood, and better health (including improved sleep and less potential for burnout).[10] You become an all-around happier, nicer, shinier version of yourself when you are grateful.

Practising gratitude can extend your life expectancy most likely because it reduces stress levels. Some studies have shown that patients that expressed gratitude two weeks after a coronary event had healthier hearts.[11] It promotes optimism and how confident a person feels about potential life outcomes.[12] [13] It can also enhance

---

10 Mills, Paul J., et al. "The role of gratitude in spiritual well-being in asymptomatic heart failure patients." Spirituality in clinical practice 2.1 (2015): 5.

11 Huffman, Jeff C., et al. "Design and baseline data from the Gratitude Research in Acute Coronary Events (GRACE) study." *Contemporary clinical trials* 44 (2015): 11-19.

12 Huffman, Jeff C., et al. "Feasibility and utility of positive psychology exercises for suicidal inpatients." *General hospital psychiatry* 36.1 (2014): 88-94.

13 Lambert, Nathaniel M., et al. "A changed perspective: How gratitude can affect sense of coherence through positive reframing." *The Journal of Positive Psychology* 4.6 (2009): 461-470.

peace of mind, and has a negative effect on depressive symptoms.[14] It is the fastest way to magically experience the full state of vitality and health you are meant to have in your body, mind, and soul.

Science also shows that practising gratitude can help you bounce back quicker after a traumatic event. Research has shown that those who practised gratitude after the September 11th attacks experienced fewer PTSD symptoms.[15] When we take our lives for granted, we don't see the good around us. When you are grateful for what you do have right now, you see life differently through a positive, abundant lens.

Practising Gratitude

"Be thankful for what you have; you'll end up having more. If you concentrate on what you don't have, you will never, ever have enough."

— Oprah Winfrey

On my journey to spiritual awakening, I practised gratitude morning and night. I deliberately sought out things to be happy for, down to the smallest detail: thank you for clean water, thank you for the cotton my shirt is made from, thank you for the spoon I stir my tea with. I intentionally raised my vibration by feeling gratitude for everything I have and have had.

Think of all the love, time, care, and money you have had spent on you. These are all things to be grateful for. When you are grateful

14 Liang, Hongyu, et al. "Mediating effects of peace of mind and rumination on the relationship between gratitude and depression among Chinese university students." *Current Psychology* (2018): 1-8.

15 Updegraff, John A., Roxane Cohen Silver, and E. Alison Holman. "Searching for and finding meaning in collective trauma: results from a national longitudinal study of the 9/11 terrorist attacks." *Journal of personality and social psychology* 95.3 (2008): 709.

for even the smallest things (time with your family or friends, seeing your kids grow, a compliment, the leaves changing colour, the sun shining), *this* is what is important in life. Your mindset becomes positive, and you attract more into your life to be positive about. I continually look up and say thank you for the beautiful sky, the stars, the abundance of nature around me, my car, the petrol, the technology that made the petrol from the oil, the people that discovered the oil, the people who developed the technology that creates cars, and so on.

Practising gratitude must become a new part of your routine if you want to receive the many rewards of living as your most awesomely fabulous self. *It is not an attitude, it is a practice*—one that requires you to be extremely deliberate. When you practice gratitude daily, you will start to notice that negativity tends to disappear as you become more grateful for where you are in life. You can rewire your brain to see the positives over the negatives.

One of the most powerful ways to practise gratitude is by journaling. You can also practise gratitude by saying it out loud in the form of prayer or through meditation. The more you do this, the more you will look for positive experiences. It then becomes part of your daily routine.

Exercise

Start each day by writing down ten things you are grateful for and *why*. Tell yourself that you will be intentionally practising gratitude each day. The more you do this, the more you will start to act in ways that confirm it. You could even give yourself themes each day. It could be finding things about your home you're thankful for, or the weather, or nature, or your spouse, or your kids. Just ask yourself what you are grateful for right now.

Do you see how you can find so much gratitude in even just the smallest things? You'll be grateful for everything, and your life will fill with colour and happiness because of it.

Night-Time Gratitude

Just before you go to sleep at night, practising gratitude helps calm down the brain. The subconscious holds on to this, helping you sleep better, and takes these calmer feelings into the next day. Studies have found that writing a gratitude journal before bed improved the duration and quality of sleep, compared to the sleep of those that didn't.[16]

Even just spending five to ten minutes reflecting on your day either with your eyes closed, or writing down what you are grateful for, has a magical ability to make you feel peaceful and relaxed. 'Are you grateful for an easy journey to work? A beautiful day? That meeting going well? The kids doing their chores? What gave you pleasure today? Did you receive any pure good fortune? What did you achieve today? Where did you express kindness today?

Finding Gratitude in Life's Challenges

> ***"Let us rise up and be thankful. For if we didn't learn a lot today, at least we learnt a little. And if we didn't learn a little, at least we didn't get sick. And if we got sick, at least we didn't die. So, let us all be thankful."***
>
> ***— Buddha***

Although it might be easy to be grateful for the good in your life, your true power lies in being grateful for the most difficult times.

16 Wood, Alex M., et al. "Gratitude influences sleep through the mechanism of pre-sleep cognitions." *Journal of psychosomatic research* 66.1 (2009): 43-48.

Everything in life is a lesson to learn from; your life is always reflecting how you feel back to you. When you experience difficult times, ask yourself what the lesson was. Discovering what you learnt is something to be grateful for. It's finding the silver lining amongst the chaos. This is where you grow as a person.

I'm grateful for a near carjacking. I'm grateful for an abusive ex-husband. *Thank you for showing me what I don't want in my life.* This helped me become a truer, more authentic version of myself.

The Latin saying "*amor fati*" means "to love one's fate". When we love our fates, we love whatever happens to us—the lesson taught. In that, we can find gratitude. Fear just holds us back, but it is impossible to feel fear with gratitude, so it helps you move into that place of love.

If someone you love becomes ill and gets better, be grateful for this and their healing. If they get sick and die, whilst you might grieve the loss, say thank you for their life and what they brought to the world, that you had the pleasure of knowing them.

Pay It Forward

When we contribute to the greater good, the collective consciousness we are all part of, it feels good. Pay it forward by donating items you don't need to charity or donating a sum of money each month. Can you buy groceries for an elderly neighbour or a family in need? Check in on loved ones and send messages of love and support? This might just remind you of how much you have to be grateful for.

The more you appreciate life and the abundance that surrounds you, the more you will find it.

Practising Gratitude for What You Want in Life

When you think about the life you want, grateful to know it's on its way, it *supercharges* your energy to attract it into your life. Dispenza says, "We have been conditioned to think we need a reason for joy, or a motivation to feel gratitude, grounds to be in a state of love." Again, this heavily relies on the external world to make us feel different internally. Instead, when you start to feel that vibration of love, joy and gratitude now, this power attracts like energy. By intentionally feeling gratitude for the life you want, you can rewire your mind and condition your body as if you already have it, thanks to those higher vibrational feelings. If you spend your time thinking about all the wonderful things you can be happy about, the universe will naturally respond to that vibration and bring you even more. It is a simple daily exercise that costs you nothing but can make an incredible difference in creating your magnificent life.

Wallis Wattle, who wrote *The Science of Getting Rich* (1910), says that gratitude is right at the heart of wealth, or anything it is you want. When you start tracking and saying thank you, money starts circulating. It's like gold dust; you're opening yourself up for more. *You will never receive what you don't appreciate.* You need to *appreciate to appreciate.* Give thanks in order to receive.

The lasting effects of gratitude are massive; you feel lighter, calmer, happier, and more confident. When you practice gratitude, you proactively look for things to be excited and grateful for—even small stuff. Gratitude amplifies everything. It's like an underrated superpower that can help change your life and alter your mental lens.

You cannot experience another frequency without being shown what you don't desire—be grateful for this. Being grateful starts as a practice and then becomes a way of life.

PART 2

ALIGNMENT

8

Values And Needs: Discovering What Matters To You Most

"It's not hard to make decisions, once you know what your values are."

— Roy E Disney

Welcome to the second part of your empowerment journey—Alignment. Now that you have discovered who you are, it's time to align what you want with what your soul desires. This means finding clarity on what's uniquely important to you, discovering your purpose, and what you're here to do and serve. This is what brings meaning to life. You will learn the skills to cleverly curate the life of your dreams and the magic of manifesting; when it's done from love, you can't help but create the life of your dreams because it's in alignment with your truth.

What Are Values?

Everyone has a value system, and this is as unique to you as your fingerprint. What matters to one person will be completely different from another. They are the principles you personally believe to be important to you, helping you choose the direction of your life so you can live to your fullest potential.

Our value system is often conditioned and formed from deep-seated beliefs, coding, and programming from our environment—whilst our true authentic values might be buried deep under what we think *should* be important to us. You might believe you are living in accordance with what's important to you, but if those values aren't yours, that will create an undercurrent of unhappiness, and you'll be unable to pinpoint why. When you live aligned to your authentic values, life flows so much easier, because you're in harmony with your soul's desires. These values then help determine the priorities in your life, allowing you to go after your dreams. They act as a yardstick to measure yourself against when you feel out of integrity, and underpin your thoughts, feelings, and behaviour—so they really have the power to help you design the life you want. This is what *you* consider important, as a unique, individual person. It's what your soul craves to be in alignment with, so you effortlessly fulfil your desires instead of living within the confines of your perception.

"Happiness is that state of consciousness which proceeds from the achievement of one's values."

—Ayn Rand

When we see others with an "easy life", it's often because they live in accordance with their values. When the opposite occurs, and your reality doesn't match your authentic values, that's when things feel "off". This can be a real source of unhappiness and helplessness, ploughing you back into victimhood. This is why it is so crucial to identify what your values are, to discover if they are even yours before you start charting your journey through life.

Values are not just all those positive, supportive traits we want the world to see. Those darker parts of us also need to be respected, heard, and accepted as you go through the process of peeling back the layers to discover and celebrate the real you.

Where Do Values Come From?

Values are intrinsically part of us and gained from life experiences, the environment you grew up in and what you heard growing up—hence why many values are inauthentic. Though you may have core "master" values, which might be fairly stable throughout life, other values might also come and go as you progress through different chapters of your life. What was important to you earlier in life might be different from what is important now.

It's not always easy to live according to our authentic value system, especially when it's muddied with programming and coding. This brings us back to not feeling safe to be our true selves. What you think you value might actually be your parents' values, or the society or culture you live in—that is, the environment influencing you. We might be so heavily imprinted with others' beliefs that we don't even know our true values. Knowing your true, unique values is of extreme importance on your journey to discovering you, because once you know, they provide the footprint on which to build your magnificent life. Just like a house needs a strong foundation, your authentic values act as the underpinning to the life *only you* have the divine ability to create.

For example, if you work a forty-five-hour week, you might believe that working hard is part of life, life is a bit of a struggle, and money is to be revered. Thus, one of your values might be hard work. Deep down, there is an adventurous and fun side to you that you continue to ignore. You're exhausted and have no time for leisure activities that your soul craves. You see others taking time out to do all sorts of fun activities, but you don't perceive this is available to you. You judge others for having fun, and this creates internal disharmony, stress, and conflict. If you don't really value winning or competition but you work in a highly corporate, sales-driven environment, you are likely to feel dissatisfied with your job. (This was actually how I was, and a major reason why I always felt a permanent knot of stress in my stomach). If you truthfully value success, accomplishment, and excellence, being a full-time mom to small children might create frustration and make you feel under-stimulated. In these types of situations, knowing your true values can really help guide you, as you can then apply a conscious awareness of what really matters to you. Then you can make decisions from a place of love, so you are intentionally creating a joy-filled existence, in alignment with your values.

One of the most incredible things about waking up and living consciously was realising that many of my values didn't belong to me. But was it safe to start living in accordance with what was truly important to me? As I child, I never felt good enough. I was jealous of others, I craved approval, and my parents always seemed busy—all of which created stress. I tried to fit in, often feeling ostracised by others. At the same time, I thought I had to work hard to achieve anything. My values were all over the place! When you start pouring awareness on this, you realise how most of what we carry around is complete nonsense. It isn't your truth at all. When you choose to no longer live with those values, that is when you create magic.

Authentic Values

When you live authentically, in accordance with your values, you feel fulfilled. Life flows with ease, confidence, joy, and purpose because you are aligning with your soul imprint.

When you think about your values, you must listen inside to see whether they *feel* right to you, knowing yourself and what's really important. Know that it is safe to realise and accept your real values. They are yours, no one else's. Just keep asking yourself to listen for what feels right with your soul. Journaling and meditation can be highly effective tools here.

Values Exercise

First, ask yourself what is important to you in life. What do you enjoy doing? When do you feel satisfied and fulfilled? What values come to mind when you think of this? Using the table of values on the next page, write a list in your journal of all the values that resonate with you. Don't analyse it too much, and don't rush this process. Be mindful not to criticise yourself here. Keeping in touch with your values is a lifelong exercise, so it is a good one to revisit (especially if you are feeling unbalanced from time to time and you can't figure out why).

When you consider each value, ask yourself:

- Is this mine, my parents, society's, or what I think I should have?
- Why do I have this value?
- Was I taught this value?
- Where did it come from?
- What is the benefit of holding this value?
- Does it excite me to make decisions aligned with this value?
- How do I feel when I think of this value? Does it make me feel good?
- Where do I embody this value in my life?
- Do I judge myself for having this value? If so, why?

Values Table

Acceptance	Faith	Perfection
Accomplishment	Fame	Personal Expression
Accountability	Family	Planning
Accuracy	Family Happiness	Play
Achievement	Famous	Pleasure
Adaptability	Fast Pace	Positivity
Advancement	Fearless	Potential
Adventure	Ferocious	Power
Affection	Fidelity	Practicality
Alertness	Fitness	Preparedness
Altruism	Focus	Present
Ambition	Foresight	Productivity
Amusement	Freedom	Professionalism
Arts	Friendship	Prosperity
Assertiveness	Fun	Privacy
Awareness	Generosity	Purity
Balance	Genius	Purpose
Beauty	Giving	Quality
Belonging	Goodness	Radiance
Boldness	Grace	Realistic
Bravery	Gratitude	Recognition
Brilliance	Greatness	Recreation
Calm	Growth	Reflective
Capable	Happiness	Relationships
Carefulness	Hard work	Reliability
Certainty	Harmony	Religion
Challenge	Health	Reputation
Change	Helping Others	Resourcefulness

Charity	Helping Society	Respect
Clear	Holiness	Responsibility
Clever	Honesty	Restraint
Collaboration	Honour	Results oriented
Comfort	Hope	Reverence
Commitment	Humility	Risk
Common Sense	Humour	Safety & Security
Communication	Independence	Satisfaction
Community	Ingenuity	Self-control
Compassion	Imagination	Selflessness
Competence	Improvement	Self-reliance
Competition	Independence	Self-respect
Completion	Individuality	Sensibility
Concentration	Influencing Others	Sensitivity
Confidence	Innovation	Sensuality
Connectedness	Inner Harmony	Serenity
Consciousness	Inquisitive	Service
Consistency	Insightful	Sexuality
Contentment	Inspiration	Sharing
Contribution	Integrity	Shrewdness
Control	Intellect	Significance
Cooperation	Intensity	Simplicity
Conviction	Intuitive	Sincerity
Country	Involvement	Skilfulness
Courage	Joy	Smart
Courtesy	Justice	Solitude
Creativity	Kindness	Sophistication
Credibility	Knowledge	Spark
Curiosity	Leadership	Speculation
Decisiveness	Learning	Spirituality
Dedication	Legacy	Spontaneity

Democracy	Liberty	Stability
Dependability	Logic	Status
Determination	Love	Strategic
Development	Loyalty	Strength
Design	Magnificence	Structure
Devotion	Making a Difference	Success
Devoutness	Mastery	Support
Dignity	Maturity	Surprise
Diligence	Meaningful Work	Sustainability
Discipline	Ministering	Talent
Discretion	Moderation	Teamwork
Discovery	Money	Temperance
Diversity	Morality	Teaching
Drive	Motivation	Tenderness
Environmental	Mystery	Thankfulness
Economic Security	Nature	Thoroughness
Education	Obedience	Thoughtfulness
Effectiveness	Openness	Timely
Efficiency	Optimism	Thrill
Elegance	Order	Tolerance
Empathy	Organisation	Toughness
Empower	Originality	Traditionalism
Endurance	Passion	Tranquillity
Energy	Patience	Transparency
Enjoyment	Peace	Trust
Enlightenment	Perfection	Truth
Entertainment	Persistence	Understanding
Enthusiasm	Personable	Unity
Equality	Personal Development	Usefulness
Ethics	Pertinent	Variety
Excellence	Philanthropic	Victory

Excitement	Placid	Vision
Exhilaration	Playful	Vitality
Experiment	Pleasant	Wealth
Expertise	Polite	Welcoming
Exploration	Popular	Winning
Expressiveness	Quality	Wisdom
Fairness		Wonder

Refs: Positivepsychology.com/Louise-Anne Maurice/Scott Jeffrey

Now, looking at your list, start compartmentalising them into groups and prioritize the value in each group that feels the most right to you. Then make a list of your most important ones. Do these feel right to you? It needs to light you up on the inside when you think about it—that's how you'll know it's an authentic value.

Now, think about what each of the values mean to you and why they are important to you. For example:

Value: Authenticity.

Means to me: Being truthful and honest in everything I do, say, and feel.

It's important because: I live my life with true integrity, in alignment with who I am, in a conscious and awakened state. This brings internal joy to my life.

When you start making value-based choices, though it might not feel safe initially, you are operating from truth. This, in time, will feel much more aligned than operating from a fear-based, egocentric mindset. You'll know because you no longer question yourself. If it makes you feel good about yourself, it's from an expansive state, because it is aligned with who you really are. When you consider your values in decision-making, you have a sense of integrity and know what is right, approaching decisions with confidence and acceptance.

Now reflect on those different domains of your life—your dreams and desires. Are you embodying your values in those different areas of your life? If not, why? When you're not, this indicates a deviation between the type of person you want to be and the type of person you are being. Again, this is okay. By pouring awareness on these discrepancies, you're highlighting more of what you want to embody. Life is one long journey of self-improvement, including acting in line with our values.

Darker Values

To live in alignment with who we are in our souls, we must stop denying those darker parts of ourselves—the ones we hide away. To be your true, magnificent self, you must work with them in loving and supportive ways. They are still part of us. Otherwise, these darker parts can conflict with your true values and prevent you from reaching your dreams.

Afraid	Guilty	Pathetic
Anger	Gullible	Poor
Angst	Hopeless	Rejected
Anxious	Hurt	Sad
Ashamed	Ignored	Selfish
Bored	Inconsequential	Sceptical
Confused	Inferior	Serious
Curious	Irritated	Stressed
Defeated	Isolate	Stubborn

Defensive	Jealous	Tense
Depressed	Lonely	Terrified
Discontented	Lost	Threatened
Discouraged	Meaningless	Tired
Disgusted	Miserable	Underestimated
Dominated	Morbid	Unhappy
Exhausted	Moribund	Uninspired
Flat	Out of Control	Useless
Flustered	Outrage	Weak
Frightened	Overwhelmed	Withdrawn
Frustrated	Panic-Stricken	Worried

Refs: New Insights Coaching

Go through the above list and write down all those darker parts of you. Again, put them into common groups so you can find the one that resonates with you most. Work through the exercise as before, to see whether they are yours or from an imprint given to you by the environment. For example, maybe you're not jealous or angry—it was just learned behaviour from your caregivers. Maybe you're not pathetic but it was something you were told repeatedly by your parents if they perceived something you were doing as "weak". Our parents were just victims of victims; they really didn't know any better.

Knowing and respecting these darker values helps you accept and love your true whole self. There's no judgement here, just awareness and acceptance so you live from authenticity instead of denying parts of you that will never bring happiness.

Basic Human Needs

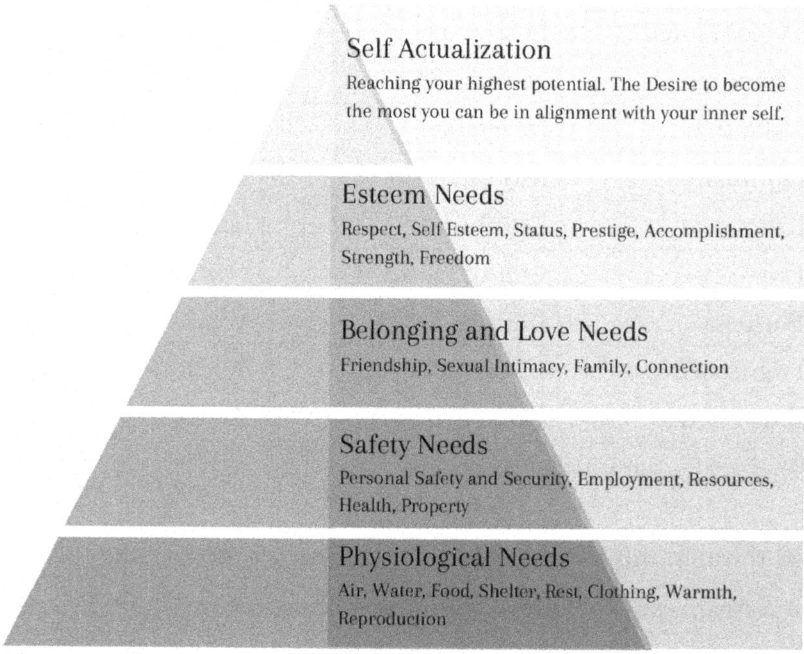

Maslow's Hierarchy of Needs

Although we have authentic values that must be embodied in our lives, human beings also have significant needs that must be met to help cultivate feelings of freedom and joy.

Maslow's Hierarchy of Needs is a well-known psychological concept that helps give a purposeful and authentic meaning to life. According to Maslow, in his "Theory of Motivation", humans have five main basic needs, which are a mixture of physiological, material, and psychological. It is not possible to live in one specific part of the triangle; all must be in sync with one another. The bottom parts of the triangle represent the support you need for life—physiological and safety needs—whereas the top is you living to the potential inside of you and the freedom you seek. In the modern world, humans place too much energy on the bottom parts, but when you live with awareness and consciousness, your focus is more on the top three: love and belonging, esteem, and self-actualization (i.e., becoming the best you can be; living in line with your highest self). When you focus closer to the top of the triangle, this is a life lived in harmony—living according to exactly who you are. This new approach focuses on what we long for (freedom), by embodying our authentic values so we can arrange our priorities accordingly.

Significant Needs

Even by focusing higher up in the triangle, humans *individually* put a different emphasis on what's important to them. The needs you consider to be of highest priority will ultimately shape your every thought, action, and behaviour which will ultimately drive your success (or failure) in life. By understanding and appreciating how your significant needs govern your choices, this will help you know yourself better and discover what you need from life.

1. Certainty

All humans need a degree of certainty and security (as Maslow pointed out). Certainty gives our lives safety, security, and predictability, helping us to avoid danger and keeping us with the familiar. We like predictability; we want to feel secure in our day-to-day lives and know our basic needs are being met. Resourceful behaviours of certainty include rituals, being organised, or having confidence in yourself. Some people value it highly, but too much certainty can lead us to want to control all aspects of our lives, so there is no risk or nasty surprises. Unresourceful behaviours include trying to control others, procrastinating, or obsessive-compulsive behaviour. Being too safe and secure creates rigidity and a fixed mindset—you can't grow or evolve. We live in a world where change is the *only* constant, so if your life becomes uncertain (and this is the human experience; we don't have complete control over our lives), this can make you feel anxious, stressed, and out of control. You can't build businesses or have fulfilling relationships with a fixed mindset. This is you living in the safety zone, being stuck and uncomfortable, scared of trying new things for fear of failure. Look at the various domains of your life and decide where certainty is serving you and where it might be holding you back.

2. Variety

Too much certainty can lead to boredom, demotivation and apathy. When you're bored, you might start acting in extreme ways in an attempt to inject some fun into your life. You might undertake risky behaviours such as taking drugs, drinking too much, or seeking out conflicts to make you feel excited. While humans need stability, we also crave the change and stimulation variety brings. Otherwise, life is too predictable. Variety invigorates us, and you can incorporate this into your life by creating new challenges, embracing new opportunities, or being creative. However, too much variety or uncertainty can trigger fear; there is too much change. It's all about hitting the sweet spot between the two needs, so life is an adventure but also safe and secure. If you're feeling bored, what can you do to add variety to your life and reap the rewards of the challenges it brings? Do you just do the same old things out of habit and safety, or do you seek the thrills? If you're craving too much variety and acting extremely, where can you find the balance in different parts of your life, so you still feel a thrill but also feel grounded and act responsibly?

3. Significance

At our core, we all want to feel approved, accepted, and loved. Thus, feeling significant is a key human need. We want to be special, distinguish ourselves, and make a difference. Being of significance, however, can be positive or negative. When it's positive, you contribute to the world, being a shining example of how to make the world a better place. When this comes from an inner desire to be a leading light and make an impact, it is driven from truth and your soul. The problem is, we live in a world where the need to feel significant is fuelled by fear and the emotional wounds of unworthiness. Therefore, we desperately search for significance, mistaking it for love and approval, and it becomes destructive and leads us to feel disconnected. Think of social media and how it feeds into a false sense of approval and love. Likes, follows, and comments are all about feeling validated by random people. This isn't you feeling love and filling up your cup, this is a desperate need to feel significant.

According to author and motivational speaker Tony Robbins, 90 percent of people place significance high up in their human needs, but that's why humans remain in victimhood. It's reactionary; you only feel significant when the outside world leaves nice comments on your filtered pictures or videos. This isn't empowerment, it's letting others determine how you feel. It might make you feel good in the moment, but before you know it, the cycle continues, and you'd do anything to make yourself feel significant and validated again. You don't have to look too far to see the number of depression and suicide cases that are linked to social media use. Ultimately, there will always be someone more significant than us. When we place too much emphasis on the need to feel significant, humans become separate from each other, and it's this separation that creates many of the problems in the world. It's fuelled by arrogance and desperation, causing us to seek external validation rather than what is important: love and connection.

4. Connection and Love

This leads nicely to the need for connection. Human beings are not meant to live separately. We are designed to connect and vibrate at that high energy frequency, feeling love for others as well as love for ourselves. Everyone innately needs some level of connection (although some people need it more than others). We want to feel part of a larger community. We want to be loved, cared for, and supported, whether it be from partners, friends, family, or connections we make through shared interests—as well as the relationship we have with ourselves. Connection makes us feel safe, like we are part of a group (we are tribal beings after all). However, too much focus on love and connection can potentially lead to neediness, co-dependence, or people-pleasing behaviours. This can lead to resentment or a sense of martyrdom, feeding into our self-esteem or self-worth issues. Feeling connection is the opposite of feeling significant. It is a delicate balance. Think about how much you need connection. Do you feel it with yourself? Do you feel it at home, with your partner and family, or in the workplace? Is there a balance where you feel unconditionally loved as well as part of something bigger, or is feeling significant but potentially separated more important to you?

5. Growth

Human beings are designed to be curious, try new things, desire growth, and develop new skills. We would not have invented anything if this wasn't the case. By learning new skills and having new experiences—whether it's starting a new course, being creative, taking a different exercise class, or travelling to a new place on your next vacation—you stretch yourself and contribute to the expansion of the universe. This is a growth mindset. You don't always have certainty and predictability, and know how the story always must end, but growth brings an element of variety and spice into our lives. When you make progress this leads to happiness and feelings of fulfilment. You strive to know more, implement more, do more with this life you've been given. Many live with a fixed mindset, not believing they have the capacity to do more, but this just comes from fear. The bigger the risk, the bigger the success. Anything is possible, but you need a growth mindset to do it.

6. Contribution

When we know we have, inside us, the power to create anything we want, we are living in our truth, vibrating from feelings of love and harmony. This creates feelings of connection to others and love for the world. We want to contribute by bringing our gifts, talents, and skills to the world. We have an inbuilt need to help, serve, or support others in a meaningful and fulfilling way. We may think our contribution must be financial, but it can also be your knowledge, time, skills, or other resources. This might include donating items you no longer want, giving your time or expertise to causes you care about, or helping in your local community in some way. When you are only contributing out of obligation or your programming, just giving, giving, and giving will deplete you over time, triggering negative feelings of resentment or anger. Sometimes contribution isn't done from love or obligation, it's only done to get something in return—feeding into our ego and our need to feel significant once again. Your contribution must be pure and selfless and make the world a better place. When you give without getting anything out of it, it makes you feel fantastic! I call this the Go-Giver Energy!

"The fruit of love is service, the fruit of service is peace."

— Mother Theresa

Valuing and Meeting Your Needs

The way to those feelings of freedom, happiness, and fulfilment is through love and connection, growth, and contribution. You will never feel whole, complete, and fulfilled when you place too much emphasis on your need for certainty, variety, and significance. Looking back at the six significant human needs, ask yourself which ones you value the most and why. Are these needs being met? What do you need more of in your life? Do they show up in some areas and not others? Are you aware of them in your daily life? What do you do to fulfil them? When you know what's important to you, just like knowing your authentic values, it can help drive you to become the best version of yourself, essentially creating a better life for you.

9

Discovering Your Purpose And Passion: Uncovering The Reason For Your Existence

"The mystery of the human existence lies not just in staying alive, but in finding something to live for."

— Fyodor Dostoyevsky

As we reach mid-life, thoughts of "What am I meant to be doing?" or "What's my purpose?" start to surface in our minds more often. Questions such as "Am I living purposefully? Am I fulfilled?" or darker thoughts like "What if I am meant to be living a completely different life?" might come to mind. These thoughts float around in our minds, refusing to go away or quiet down, subtly nudged by that increasingly loud inner voice that wants to be heard. We are aware that the years pass by, and we fear missing out on life. We have gained more life experience, knowing what we think we like, but we are more exposed to death. We see our family and friends ageing, loved ones passing on. Sometimes those close to us in age die due to illnesses we perceive only "older" people get (cancer, Alzheimer's, heart disease, osteoporosis, etc.). This can properly wake us up as it becomes laser clear that we aren't here forever (at least, not physically). Recognising this helps remind us that life is short, fragile, and precious. By allowing yourself to live purposefully and with fulfilment, you bring clarity to the amazing life you can create, just as were divinely designed to do. When you discover your purpose—

your "why", this is what fuels you through life. Finding your purpose and embodying it fully means you won't look back with regret.

"The things that bring you the greatest joy are in alignment with your purpose."

– Jack Canfield

When you live purposefully, this expands to all areas of your life, giving them meaning and integrity. Research conducted by Jodi L Berg showed that when you move from self-interested goals to more contributive goals for the greater good, your motivations and thoughts change, and you grow more as an individual.[17] Human beings are designed to be purpose-driven creations, to be co-creators with the universe, to help the world expand. Most people regret the things they didn't do—rather than the things they did.

Every experience we have—the good, the bad, and everything in between—is there to teach us something and help draw us back to our true path. Every single person on the planet can find their purpose if they are prepared to. In doing so, you must embrace fear as you come up against new challenges, and be prepared to listen to yourself whether it feels right for you or not. This builds self-confidence and a determination to discover your purpose and act on it. *We all have a superpower—you just have to go find it.*

"What a blessing it is that you're even here
— yes the miracle of life that you exist —
you got this opportunity, you got something, give love for it,
contribute for it, earn it, give for it. You're still here for a reason."

— Wayne Dyer

---

17 Berg, Jodi L. "The Role of Personal Purpose and Personal Goals in Symbiotic Visions." April 2015.

If you want to experience life in the most amazing magical awe-inspiring way—you need to do it from a place of purpose. As conscious-living activist Jacey Graham says of purpose-work: "It's as if life was all written out with a convenient list of tick boxes. I did everything on the list—went to school, got a qualification, had fun with my friends, tried a few people on for size, met a boy, married him, had a career, travelled the world, had three kids, and then suddenly after the distractions of what the external world said I was 'meant to do' died down, it was like the author ran out of ink. Now what?" We spend so much of our life worrying about what *we think we want;* we miss the signs of who we actually are designed to be. Living consciously invites you to go inwards and ask the question of who we are and what we are designed to be so we don't miss opportunities, signals, and messages showing us what our true purpose is. You'll know when you find your purpose, because you'll live feeling fulfilled. Life is easy!

Don't deny others your gifts. Living without your purpose is the opposite of living authentically and won't bring you the joy and freedom you crave. Once you have opened your mind to living consciously and fulfilled, you will want to find and live according to your purpose, and you'll keep on going until you find it.

Living in accordance to your purpose will motivate and propel you along as you curate the life of your dreams, but sometimes it might cause you to be stuck in a place of frustration or even fear when you can't figure it out. Your purpose is fluid and may change as you walk your path through life. This might take you by surprise, especially when we make sudden diversions, such as a massive career change, ending a relationship, relocating, or taking a different life direction. It might take time to find out what your real purpose is, but that is what the universe wants for us: to feel different experiences and *hone our preferences* until we find the ones that allow us to feel the high-frequency energy vibrations at which we were designed to exist. The more you listen within, to your soul, the more you will find your purpose. Listen to that authentic inner voice, pleading with you to go find what it is you're meant to be doing.

Ask yourself what you understand by the word "purpose". What does it mean to you? Do you feel your life is one of purpose?

The dictionary definition of purpose is "the reason for which something is done or created, or for which something exists". It also means "doing something with determination and intention", because when you live consciously, you make it your mission to feel fulfilled and live in your truth. *Purpose work should be one of the biggest investments you can make in yourself.* It says you matter, you're of value, you have a gift the world needs. When you live with purpose, you intentionally grab life by the hands and thrive because you're connecting to who you are inside. This creates direction and helps leave the world a better place. It might be that you are here to teach, or to look after others, or to make great discoveries that impact the world. Maybe your talent is to delight people with your music, cooking, artistic skills, quick analytical mind, or compassion. Maybe your purpose originates from a place of pain or lack. It's often your story that helps guide and ignite you. Neither is right or wrong, and you can only be aligned with who you are, not what you think you should be doing. You just need to find it and go and execute it to your highest potential. As Eckhart Tolle points out, "Your inner purpose is to awaken. It's as simple as that. Finding and living in alignment with the inner purpose is the foundation to fulfilling your outer purpose. It is the basis for true success."

What If I Don't Find My Purpose?

When you don't live a life of purpose, this creates feelings of unfulfillment. It's why those that rise to the top feel unfulfilled and dissatisfied. *It's the biggest waste to achieve "success" but not fulfilment.* This is why those that have accumulated masses of wealth don't feel happy. Worse, it's why those in the spotlight often take their own lives because achievement, wealth, and fame didn't bring what they craved: freedom and fulfilment. Success without fulfilment is the ultimate failure. Anyone can be successful, but *only you* can discover what fulfils you. The world needs you to be *you*, with all the unique gifts and skills you bring to the world.

When you don't find your purpose, you drift, like a small dinghy bobbing up and down in the middle of the ocean. You're not exactly in grave danger, but you do lack direction. Sometimes it might feel quite peaceful, but other times you feel a bit lost, disorientated, and frustrated that you're not reaching a destination. The longer you stay bobbing around, contemplating your frustrations with the world, the longer you stay stuck, feeling discouraged that you're not living a life of ease and joy. Your values feel compromised, and you feel a disconnect with your inner self. What you'd really like right then is for a rope to be thrown to you by that bigger boat going past, the one who seems to know where they are going. But the captain of that bigger boat is actually you—your inner self. Only you can navigate that vessel with courage, bravery, and determination to where you are meant to be.

Discovering Your Purpose

Some people just know their purpose, don't they? This can be extremely triggering if you are pretending that your life is fulfilled but feeling the opposite. Even in childhood you might have heard those kids that said, "I'm going to be a doctor when I grow up", or "I want to be an engineer", or "I want to be a teacher". Or the kids whose commitment was outside of modern-day measures of success and academia, racking up medals, accomplishments, and recognition.

Those people used to irk me. I thought I must have missed the memo on what I was meant to be doing. I was judgmental and critical of their drive, determination, capability, and self-belief, and let them make me feel small because I didn't have a clue. Many of us don't know our purpose, and we often must reach a state of burnout, crisis or tragedy before people wake up and start living a meaningful fulfilled life. When I took responsibility for my life, showered myself with self-love and forgiveness, I recognised that all my choices were part of a much bigger plan. One which was leading me to where I was meant to be: a place of awareness, consciousness, and ultimately sharing this knowledge with others.

Everything I experienced was a lesson to gently guide me back to what I was divinely meant to be doing. I'd gotten a degree in Economics and done nothing with it. I worked in sales for ten years and felt I'd *sold my soul,* never truly living in alignment with my values. I retrained as a nutritional therapist, thinking that was my purpose, but all it did was make me feel like I'd lost my integrity each time I allowed myself to eat something not especially healthy. I was meant to experience it all, this was my life's path, so now I look back at it all with gratitude. My degree taught me how to write and be analytical. My ten years in recruitment meant I could empathise, listen, and figure out what people wanted. My nutritional therapy skills taught me the confidence to teach others. Only when I chose to listen did I then experience the unfoldment of what I was meant to be doing.

"Doing what you love is the cornerstone of having abundance in your life."

— Wayne Dyer

The Process of Finding Your Purpose

The very act of listening within will help guide you to your purpose. It isn't anyone else's, so when you dive deeply here, you need to be aware of any programming and a blueprint telling you what you think you should be doing versus what you authentically want. Let go of doubt, trust yourself, and be determined to cultivate the best version of yourself all whilst forgiving and releasing the past. As the saying goes: Forgive your younger self, believe in your current self, create your future self.

Start by asking yourself these reflective questions:

- What hobbies, skills, talents, and gifts do you have? Look back over your life and write them down. I guarantee you have a lot!
- What did you most enjoy doing when you were growing up?
- What would your parents say you were like as a child?
- What lights you up? What turns you on? What really makes you excited?
- What are your unique key strengths? Have any of these come from challenging situations?
- What do you do that leaves others feeling better than before?
- If you had unlimited time, money, or resources, what would you spend your life doing? Who would you be with? What would life look like?
- What does your perfect day look like? Really think about what you would do if you were given twenty-four hours to do whatever you wanted? You could mind-map this, so you make sure you don't miss anything. Again, this is what you *want* to do, not what you think you *should* do.
- What could you easily talk to people about for thirty minutes, with no preparation?
- What do you most enjoy doing? What makes time just disappear, puts a smile on your face, and makes you feel content and in flow?
- What is your favourite topic of conversation? (If it's you, that's okay. Just make sure it's from a loving space, not your

ego talking and needing attention.)

- What would your epitaph say?
- Who or what inspires you? Why?
- What are your superpowers? What are you good at?
- What would you like to do in the future? In five years? Ten years? Twenty?
- What would you like to do before you die?
- What would the world lose if you didn't exercise your purpose?
- What would you like your loved ones to say at your funeral?
- What would you like to be remembered for?
- Think about all areas of your life from the life domain on page 32. Do you want that house by the sea? The size-six clothes? The relationship? The job? The wealth? What feelings do these evoke? Why do you want them?
- What impact or legacy would you like to leave in the world?

Now ask how you can start intentionally weaving these answers into your daily life. As Jim Carrey says, "Intention is everything. Everything is from this. Nothing happens without. Not one single thing happens without it." How can you carve out an hour each day to do something you love doing? Can you book a dance class? Can you sign up for an online course? Can you start that project you've been desperate to do? Who do you know who has done this? Who seems to effortlessly live their purpose?

A major part of my purpose is writing this book to help raise the collective consciousness of others, so you can live truthfully, powerfully, joyfully, and *free*! Sometimes it might take others living their purpose to prompt you into action, which was the case for me. I procrastinated for about a year before writing this book, subconsciously finding reasons not to write even when I'd told my coach, bestselling author and motivational speaker Sanae Floyd, this was the plan. It became that aggravating, unfulfilled dream at the back of my head—something unavailable to me. It wasn't until I spoke to a potential client about the books she had written but never published out of fear of not being good enough that I had that lightbulb moment. I thought, "Uh oh, that will be me, full of regret for never doing it." In that moment, I told myself repeatedly I would write this book, it felt incredible in my soul, and the universe listened. It sent opportunities, events, and people that would allow this to happen into my path, *like magic.*

When you live in your truth, it's your soul that will pull you forward. The soul is your inner compass, guiding you on the path to fulfilment. Many will never listen because of self-doubt and a fear of failure. Trust your feelings; they never lie. If you've been ignoring things you want to do or feel pulled towards, you must start listening now. Time will pass anyway. Are you going to go and pursue your purpose and make that positive impact by sharing your gift to the world?

If you struggle with this, ask yourself these questions:

- Why am I resistant to listening to myself?
- Why is it safer to live with self-limiting beliefs than my truth?
- Who will I upset if I start to live as my authentic self?
- What are the hidden benefits to never finding my purpose (you might think it's hard so easier not to try, or you don't have the right skills to do it so at least you don't have to fear failure)?
- Can I forgive and love myself through the "mistakes" I have made?

Trusting the Process

Life will always throw curveballs in our direction—that's how it works *so we can learn and evolve*. It is an art and skill to be able to observe and practice accepting what is, being objective and curious of what is being shown instead of being reactive. When challenges are presented, it's easy to slip back into victimhood, making us contract and limiting our ability to have a clear vision of what our life experiences are all about. The beautiful thing about growth is that for the new to emerge, you must make space by releasing the old. You might not understand the current obstacle, but it will become clear. Be resolute and trust the process even when your ego is screaming the opposite. The more you learn, the more clarity you feel.

High Vibe Tribe

"Align yourself with people that you can learn from, people who want more out of life, people who are stretching and searching and seeking some higher ground in life."

— Les Brown

If you spend your time with people who are negative and complain about what life has dealt them, it is likely you will start thinking the same. How can you possibly be passionate and purposeful about anything when you are surrounding yourself with people like that? When you become discerning about what you let into your life and surround yourself with people who have a determined vision, this keeps you on your path and challenges you to do the same. Surround yourself with people who push you to be better, who have your back unconditionally, and just want to see you succeed. Share your purpose and passion with those that are visionaries, not those who are stuck and just think life isn't in their control. Positivity is contagious, but so is negativity; you make the choice.

Managing Those That Don't Share Your Vision or Passion

It might be easy to say no to coffees or lunch dates with that friend you used to hang out with, but when it's close family members, it can be more of a challenge. You always have something to learn from those that trigger you or don't share your passion. Maybe they bring up old fears, or maybe they show you how much you don't want to be like them. If you're still reacting to this, you've still got some healing to do. That's okay, be thankful for showing you. Be mindful that judgement and criticism come from their own place of lack. It's so they feel better because your path of greatness highlights their deficiencies. When you find yourself in this situation, being self-aware is of utmost importance. Remind yourself you are safe; it is your life to lead, and you will regret it if you don't do this. This takes courage. Yes, you may upset people. Often when you shift and start to vibe at a higher frequency, those around you shift too. Where energy goes, energy flows, so the energy you give off will start to resonate at a higher frequency. Energy attracts like back, so you might just find they are in a happier space too. This is to be celebrated because you're helping to improve the frequency of others.

Second, you might just have to hold space for those who don't see or understand your brilliance. These might include those with selfish tendencies or those so wounded by life they are unable to feel unconditional love. It is as if their soul is so removed from their physical form, they can't hear their inner voice. They are unable to believe what is possible for them because they've let their mind run the show for so long. Just empathize and forgive them for how they think and behave. The best bit: your awesomeness isn't being dictated to by someone else's unconscious way of living.

Self-Connection

The more you connect with yourself, the more you're connecting with your truth. When you recognise that the most important relationship you have is the one with yourself, this helps you discover your purpose. Here are some exercises for finding that self-connection:

- Create space for "you time" in the morning. Find five non-negotiables you can do that will make you a happier person. Mine include visualisation or meditating, planning my day, cuddling my dog, doing some study or work, and exercising.
- Start (or continue) a journaling practice.
- Take intentional daily time to tune into your body. Spend five minutes a day quieting your mind and listening to your body. Are you angry, happy, sad, excited? What's going on and why? What do you need to do to pour love on yourself? Pay attention to your thoughts and emotions. Do they feel light or heavy? Are you operating from love or fear? What are you trying not to feel?
- Reconnect with your values, beliefs, and intentions. Are you living purposefully in all that you do in different areas of your life?
- Carve out time to do a short, daily self-check-in. Are you incorporating those things you love each day?
- Go do something creative.
- Implement meditation and mindfulness into your day so you practice being present and aware.
- What's good for the body is good for the soul, so exercise in some capacity each day.
- Practice reflection. Look back and remind yourself of all that you have achieved and those times you felt fulfilled.
- Look at your wants. Is your behaviour bringing you closer to them?

- Practice acceptance of what is.
- Start putting boundaries in place; work out what you want and stick to it. Say "No" to things that don't feel right.

You were put on this Earth to achieve your greatest self, to live out your purpose, and to do it courageously. If you find the process of working out what you love to do difficult, asking others might help. Those people you spend the most time with see when you are feeling high vibe, even if you don't realise it. Ask others what they think of you and what they think your skills, knowledge, and gifts are. Choose individuals you trust to have your back, or you'll be dealing with hidden judgements and criticism from those that don't support your evolution.

If you don't pursue what you love, you will feel out of alignment, resentful, and at odds with the world. However, on this magical journey of uncovering your purpose, respect that it might take time, and understand that there might be challenges and potential difficulties along the way. Knowing that you have a genuine passion or purpose is going to help you through these difficult patches. When you keep doing things that don't come naturally to you, you're going to get fed up and disillusioned.

Knowing how to find your purpose and passion in life is essential for inner happiness. Life is a never-ending journey of experience, but the search for identity, purpose, truth, and authenticity are what make the journey fulfilling. When you find your purpose, this fulfils the desire to reach peace and effortless joy. This can be challenging and scary as we constantly evolve throughout our lives. When you experience uncertainty and challenges, this also makes it difficult to find your purpose and live in your truth. When we feel stuck, but life is just moving along, this can also be a struggle. See this as an opportunity to test your strength and resolve. It doesn't change who you are deep down, it just helps to prime you for an empowered, truthful journey.

Once your purpose is clear, it is easy to get focused and not be derailed by situations, naysayers, and negativity. And it won't feel like hard work. In fact, it will feel easy and effortless.

10

Integrating Your Human Soul

"Alignment is a power, a flow, a high vibrational frequency that has your own personal identity imprinted on it."

— Oprah Winfrey

Aligning With Your Truth

The dictionary definition of *alignment* is to "bring things together in proper coordination". You might think of the stars and moon aligning or a chiropractor physically aligning your spine, but most of the world has never thought of applying it *to themselves.* So what are you meant to be aligned with? That's easy: your higher self, your soul, *your highest potential.* That voice—the one asking to be the loudest of all the voices you listen to is your authentic self talking. Living in alignment with this is all that matters, and when you intentionally design your life, making decisions in accordance with who you truly are, *that's when* you create the magnificent reality you dream of.

You were taught to believe the external world should create those magical flowy feelings for you, but now you recognise this just makes you at the mercy of others' decisions and expectations. In victimhood, fear is the dominant voice, but this keeps you firmly out of alignment. You give away your power, creating all sorts of problems—anxiety, fear, sadness, distrust, resentment, anger, and disappointment because your thinking and emotions emanate from your beliefs. None of this is real or who you actually are. The real you gets lost amongst the noise as you travel through life trying to gain love, approval and acceptance, closing yourself off to the potential that is available to you. Therefore you swing like a pendulum. You see those things you want, but you go back and forth, scared and confused, wanting one thing but doing another. *Your soul just wants you to be at peace and find freedom by living as you were designed to be. To make choices from your heart, instead of being held prisoner by your head.* To feel your way through life, to try it all on and with deep curiosity see what fits. Each time you are shown what is available, you have a choice: stay in safety and fear or discover if something feels right for your soul. Your only job is to live from this place. When you embrace this, you change your reality, because you are making choices that align your vibrations with those of the universe—the soul inside of you. From this, you will create those magical, high-vibrational feelings of peace, freedom, love, and joy you desire.

When You're Out of Alignment

You know when you are out of alignment because you feel flat and depressed. Your energy is vibrating at a low frequency. It feels heavy and dark. You'll feel that borderline misery, tired, a bit off, things not being quite right, with a slight sense of panic and stress, felt often in our stomach, chest, or throat. It's a fear-based feeling. Nothing seems to work right, and it feels like you're pushing a boulder up a hill. You feel stuck and frustrated and you don't know how to shift it. I liken it to an omnipresent, low-grade feeling of irritation. Something I used to feel often, even as a child, but couldn't put my finger on what it was. When you're out of alignment, the universe keeps sending situations and people to trigger you. Sometimes you listen and auto-correct, but most of the time, you don't. You think, "No, this who I am, this is what life looks like," hoping it will just all just sort itself out. But then you just feel that disconnect, that "unease". You don't know who you are anymore or who to listen to for advice, and you wonder why it's not possible to feel that "ease" and effortless joy you search for.

Many people choose to do the opposite of what their parents said or did thinking that's what will bring happiness, but don't be fooled into thinking this is alignment. Making decisions from here is still making them from anger and fear, driven by perception and proving others wrong. This is just you soothing your ego, not nurturing your soul.

You will feel out of alignment with any decision you make that isn't from a place of love. Whether that's big, life-changing decisions right down to the words that come out of your mouth, who you choose to spend time with, what you spend time doing, or even the choices regarding the food you eat or the clothes you wear. Self-awareness allows you to take a step back and ask yourself what is happening right now. Does this decision make you feel good? Does it make you feel light, flowy, energised, enthusiastic even—at ease? Is it a decision from the heart? Do an energetic "check up" each time. What is being shown that still needs to be processed and healed?

You will keep attracting out-of-alignment situations, people, and events in your life until you heal your wounding and emotional voids. Healing these can be painful, I know, but you will not get what you want whilst you operate from fear. Don't ignore low vibrational feelings—allow them to come to the surface so you can understand them, respect them, process and release them. Be grateful for being shown what you need to heal from so you step closer to your baseline frequency of love. I do this every time I am triggered, and not only does it increase my vibration, but I also get excited to be shown what I still need to heal from. The more it happens, the more I step closer to my true authentic self.

Remaining Out of Alignment

If you hold yourself chronically out of alignment, which many do, you will create a life of lack. Life will feel a rollercoaster ride of temporary ups and downs but never that ease and flow. Holding on to limiting beliefs that aren't true and thinking that things aren't available to you will *always* keep you out of alignment. The energy you put out there isn't reflecting what you desire because you're saying one thing (I desire this), but believing another (I can't have it), and your beliefs will always win. The energy from the beliefs you hold will always repel the manifestation of what you desire.

"The sorrow that has no vent in tears may make other organs weep."

— Henry Maudsley

It is mentally and physically exhausting to hold back your true self, out of alignment and live according to a different version of who you think you are. If we don't process our emotions or truly feel heard, stuffing down how we really feel, this can manifest as physical symptoms. Think of people like Louise Hay who wrote *You Can Heal Your Life* or Bessel Van Der Kolk, who wrote *The Body Keeps the Score*. According to Hay and Van Der Kolk, physical symptoms *always* have an emotional component. When the emotion behind the pain is resolved, the physical problem is often alleviated.

Stepping into Alignment

"When your life is aligned with who you are, deep down inside, you let go of resistance and invite in the ease and flow of life's energy. This alignment brings a clear purpose and fulfilment to your life. Make decisions aligned with your values and nourish what feels good to you."

— Sara Raymond

When you are in alignment, you believe *anything* is possible, that *you deserve that which you desire.* When you listen to the desires driven by your soul, you are in harmony with your highest self. You create thoughts that have an energetic parallel between your human and soul.

When you're in alignment, it feels like constantly being in that joyous state of love. It's as if everything you put your mind to just works because you unknowingly pull together all the conditions, opportunities and components necessary for the physical manifestation of your desires. Life feels effortless and happens in such an easy way. You feel passion and determination, an energy of enthusiasm pulling you along for what you want because it's in harmony with your soul. As Paul Coelho says, "When you want something, all the universe conspires to help you achieve it." Life becomes more fulfilling and you feel an inner contentment as you feel connection to something far greater than you.

When you know what you want, trust yourself and it feels right, you're living in truth. You were designed to easily tap into what's next when you're aligned and you have faith what you want will come because you trust the process. You let go of any attachment to the outcome or how it has to look (which is why you won't find any goal-setting exercises in this book, as this just feeds into your need for control), allowing life to flow. It's a powerful and expansive vibration. You were designed to grow and evolve. The universe says *Yes!* to everything you think, say, and do so choose to do it from a place of love—your truth.

"We are not human beings having a spiritual experience, we are spiritual beings having a human experience."

— Pierre Teilhard De Chardin

Consciously choosing to live how you were meant to means you are using your intuition to live according to your soul's desires. This is a skill you need to learn and trust because we aren't taught to live like this; we don't "trust our gut instinct". We ignore it. You're going to have to be brave, no longer scared to be your full self. It might be hard to make decisions that don't satisfy those around you. Stand firm as you step into your power, living your truth. It's *your* life, no one else's, and don't get caught up in the nonsense of who we think we "should be".

> ***"Align your personality with your purpose and no one can stop you."***
>
> ***— Oprah Winfrey***

You must apply with focus and determination the universal law of life that you can create what you want, by listening intently to your feelings to stay in alignment. It is the biggest piece of you creating your magical magnificent life. You can only align with who you actually are, not who you aspire to be. That is why it's so important to undo the self-limiting beliefs and work on your self-love. Once you have that determined desire and belief to listen to what you truly want, you'll start feeling that higher vibe shift, into who you were always designed to be.

You'll know when you're in alignment all those seemingly random "coincidences" keep on happening without any real influence from us. You need to be extremely present and conscious of these messages. When that acquaintance cancels the coffee you never really wanted to go to, or you see an advert for a destination you dream about, or you overhear a conversation about how easy it is to become qualified in whatever the dream is you hold, those synchronicities are alignment. In my case, it was hearing my name seven times in twenty-four hours. This is you being you; no longer living in the energy of obligation but stepping into that go giver energy, you feel empowered, meeting your wants and needs. As Gary Zukav says,

"Your job on Earth is to use your personality to serve the energy of your soul."

Being Intentional

"Intentions comprise the journey of your life, how you experience it in the present moment and the quality of that moment. Your dreams and wants are the desired outcomes of these intentions."

— Sara Raymond

To live aligned to who you authentically are, you must do it with intention. You might not think so, because up until now you lived on automatic, from a place of unconsciousness, but we do have full control over our intentions, desires, and dreams. It is important to solidify these intentions because when you do this, there is a new pattern of behaviour for how you think, feel, and act. You can feel the difference in your body, your energy levels, and your emotions. This is you vibrating on a higher energy frequency! As Sara Raymond says, "Control over our intentions determines how we respond to moments in life as you regularly check in to see if you are living in line with your inner self, your purpose, with your values and needs. Respond to situations skilfully and be open to possibility as they present themselves." By living in alignment with your set intentions, this builds on the foundations of your value system, your true self, and helps you design a life of ease and freedom with focus.

Examples of intentions might be "I am worthy", "I am positive", "I am focused", "I trust myself", "I live according to my wants and needs", "I listen to myself for every decision I make", or "I always trust in my higher self".

Exercise

Write three intentions that feel right to you here.

____

____

____

When you are vibrating at that high-vibe energy frequency, telling yourself how amazing you are—loving the good, the parts you hid away for so long, and all the in-between — that's when you're in alignment. Life is always unfolding; your truth can be shown, so allow it to come through. Care deeply about how you want to feel and guide your thoughts to feed your behaviour. The more you do it, the more you stay on your path. It's so powerful but provides a huge sense of relief to know that life doesn't have to be hard work. Accept, let it flow, and dare to listen to your essence in everything you do. Life is miraculous, *you* are miraculous. Don't you owe it to the universe to live your absolute best existence?

Listening to Your Intuition

We live in a high-octane, noisy world that can easily us. You've got to cut through the noise and listen inward *to your heart and soul.* As spiritual teacher Sonia Coquette says, the home of your soul is in your heart, but we are so heavily imprinted we have no idea how life is meant to work. You've got to give yourself permission and be intentional to listen to your intuition, *even if it differs from what others want.* When you make decisions, listen to your gut. Part of the nervous system called the vagus nerve runs from your brain to your gut to keep you safe, and this is that gut feeling that you pick up right there.

Exercise to listen to your intuition

(from Sonia Coquette)

Find a quiet space where you won't get disturbed. Sit or lie down with your eyes closed. Start concentrating on your breath so you can focus on the present moment and quiet the inner noise.

Start breathing in and out slowly, like you're breathing through a straw. Do this once more, then on the third breath, push the breath out of your head and into your heart. Let out a comforting "ahh". Notice where you land in your body, where you are so quiet in your body. This is that intuitive part of your body.

Then think of a question that you want your intuition to help you answer. Breath in and out a few times, and you'll get some insight. You're shifting awareness. It has to be an authentic question. If you do this ten times you will start getting this quickly. Speak it out loud to yourself. Otherwise, it stays in your head, not your heart. You can use this for *any* decision. It works! And what your heart says *will* be right.

11

Actualizing Your Magnificent Life

"Ask for what you want, and be prepared to get it."

— Maya Angelou

You can have anything you want, but it has to come from love, not from your old emotional wounds or fears. The word "manifesting" might conjure up ideas of magic or enchantment, but it really isn't. We manifest our reality *all the time* from our thoughts, our beliefs, our emotions and subsequent actions. When you are guided by your heart, the home of your soul, *then* you're in a place to start manifesting your best life. It *will* happen—as if by magic.

This "power" is beyond us, it's something bigger than us. When you live authentically, you can physically feel the energy racing around your body, as you consciously and deliberately listen to yourself when making decisions. The way you create your world will be perceived as luck or good judgement, but *this is manifesting mastery at its best.* You've made the choice to listen to that beautiful voice, living the way we were designed to, instead of the one we were taught.

When I chose to listen to my heart and started to practise self-love, I started creating what I wanted. Every day, I choose to stay in alignment with my soul. I know what makes me feel high vibes, and because that is my essence, what I want comes in. When it doesn't,

I ask what is going on. What is being shown to me? I process it instead of distracting myself and suppressing my feelings. I practice acceptance and pour love on myself instead of being impatient and disappointed. I create what I want in all areas of my life—whether that's people, love, happiness, money, confidence, vibrant health or in my business.

The Magic to Unlocking Your Magnificent Life

The magic to getting what you want is having resolute clarity, attention, intention, and focus. *Energy flows where attention goes.* Therefore, you have to clear out the nonsense, switch the noise off so you can hear, focus on what you want and why, and that is when you manifest the life you desire.

"Let the thought inform the feeling to create the energy so you manifest what you want."

— Dr Joe Dispenza

You are an energetic being, so whatever energy you are vibrating at, you will attract that reality. Each thought you have informs your feelings. This creates an energy flow into our physicality, so your behaviour and actions manifest this into your experiences whether it's what you want or not. You become what you think.

The universe is a place of unlimited possibilities and potential, and all your thoughts, feelings, dreams, and ideas are *physically out there,* just waiting to be realised. To create that incredible life you want, *it has to start with your thoughts and beliefs*. When you hold a thought that is out of alignment with what you desire, you will suffer, and everything will feel like hard work. You'll feel tired and irritated and prevent the manifestation of the very desire you want in the first place.

"Initiate a habit of choosing thoughts and ideas that support feeling good and powerful and that elevate you to a higher state of consciousness."

— Wayne Dyer

Each day, tell yourself what you want, why you want it, and that you can absolutely achieve it. Find evidence to support these new beliefs. There is a continuous supply of experience around you, you've just got to look for it. These powerful new words and thoughts have a higher vibrational frequency, taking you back to your truth. The more you do it, the more you rewire your mind to believe new things. When you catch yourself thinking darker, negative thoughts, process and accept what is being shown to you. Practice self-awareness, be curious, don't ignore it. Think, "Oh, what's that triggering me? Why am I thinking that?" Pour a huge amount of love and forgiveness on yourself, and congratulate yourself for how self-aware and observant you're being. Lower vibrations don't manifest as fast as higher vibrations, so don't fear them.

Emotions

"When the basis for your actions is inner alignment with the present moment, your actions become empowered by the intelligence of life itself."

— Eckhart Tolle

Your emotions are a clear indication of *whether what you are thinking at that moment is in alignment with the frequencies of your desire.* You will feel positive emotions from thoughts aligned to what you truly want and negative ones when you don't. They are the traffic lights—there to signal whether you should go for it or stop. *To stay in alignment is to care very deeply about how you feel.*

Go through all the desires you have. Get raw with how you want to feel. If you have that incredible relationship, will you feel passion? Excitement? Contentment? When you have the house or the money you so desire, will you experience safety, security, or peace? Instead of hoping to feel a certain way by external circumstance, ask what emotional state you need to be in *now* to create the manifestation of your desires. Get extremely specific as you drill down to what it is you want.

When you feel an emotion you don't want, the old response is to ignore it and distract yourself. You tell yourself to let it go, and think happy thoughts, but all you're doing is pushing it down because it's too painful to feel. That energetic response remains there, never fully processed, fuelling your perception and stopping you from creating your epic life. If you feel those darker emotions, this is what will feed into your *general or dominant frequency*, and you will create a reality that matches this. When you live consciously and are aware of your thoughts and feelings, you can use these unwanted emotions for your epic level-up. This awareness allows you to learn from the external world. Those things still triggering you are a reflection of what is going on inside and are there for you to heal, so you start working on the negative feelings and clear them up so you're no longer creating from that space. You'll know when they've gone because you'll feel it energetically in your body—you'll feel light again.

You control your destiny and your human experience day by day. Happiness and joy are of course the ideal vibe, but just being aware of the world and accepting that life will throw you curve balls will also create an experience. It's not all going to feel amazing all the time. Respect your low-vibe feelings. You've had a bad day? Or received bad news? Experience it fully, pour awareness on it, understand why you feel the way you do, *then* shift back into your happy gear.

You've Got to Become the Person You Want to Be

"If you don't make the commitment
to start becoming the person you need
to be to create the extraordinary life you really want,
what makes you think that tomorrow, or next week
or next month or next year is going to be any different?"

— Hal Elrod

Start living, feeling, and thinking as if you already have what you want. Then you start creating the next step. This is the most powerful way to energetically magnetize what you want because you are living in this new energy of being who you were always meant to be. Visualise your highest self and start showing up as it. *You* get to decide your future, *you* control the environment. It's already out there in the universe, the only difference is how you look at it and your deep-seated desire to get it. The more you feel the feelings of what you want, the more you believe it is on its way, the more you make space for it to happen. As Dispenza says, "becoming the person you aspire to be requires you to stop being that old self."

Start embodying all of this as if you already have what you want. Can you be that person now, without waiting for something to happen first? You don't need to wait until you're successful to feel successful. You don't need to wait until you feel loved to feel love. You don't need to wait until you feel happy to feel happy. You can become the person you were always destined to be by knowing, trusting, and loving that person inside of you, and start being that person today.

"If you can dream it, you can do it."

— Walt Disney

It might not be easy in the beginning—and yes, your brain will question what you are doing. Your subconscious will scream this isn't true, that it's delusional, but you must remind yourself that this is just the disconnect between your conscious thinking and your subconscious wanting to keep you safe. You've got to accept the unpredictability and practice acceptance of it. Your subconscious will want to keep you safe in a place of predictability so even when good stuff happens, self-doubt and disbelief might creep in.

Be aware of self-sabotage, procrastination, and the temptation to go back to your safe space. It's scary to step out of your comfort zone and you will feel the weight of it energetically. Find your way through it, respect it, and be observant. Be grateful for what is showing up for you right now, and for being shown what you don't want. Look for evidence to support this new way of thinking and believing, and you will create situations, people, and events in your life that help you create what you want. The more you do this, the more your brain starts feeling the coherence once again. When you think, feel and act as if you already have what you want, this sends a clear message to the universe and you prime your brain for your future potential to be realised.

Clarity

Being lucid and laser clear about what you want and *why* is crucial to getting what you want. Listen to yourself energetically and emotionally and see where you are applying your energy and focus. Your natural state is clarity and well-being. As a child, we knew what we wanted, but the world started saying no, so by adulthood we were just too scared to ask for what we wanted or believe it was even possible. If your desires create incredible feelings, and you're full of energy and vitality, then it's working—you're in alignment. If not, then you must go back and ask. Do you really want this, or does this desire belong to someone else? Is it blocking you from what you want? What beliefs do you hold that are preventing the manifestation of what you desire?

Exercise

Look at your life domains and work out where you judge and criticise because it might be what you truly want. You judge that woman with the effortless confidence, money in the bank, and a rewarding job—might you secretly want that too? Question your judgments; maybe you are overriding what you want due to programming. Go back to your dream life statement. Does it create those high-vibrational feelings you crave? Don't be scared. When you take risks in alignment with who you are and develop the ability to be fully present, those risks bring the greatest rewards.

Take moments of stillness, and in quiet contemplation, ask to be shown if you don't know what it is you want. Meditate on clarity or simply tell the universe you are open to being shown. Try new things—it doesn't matter if you discover that they're not right for you. This just keeps helping you filter down to what you do want. Let go of the meaning you give it all. You'll know when it feels right. Keep your eyes and ears open for signs that come into your path. Your soul wants your physical being to experience everything so you find what's right. You might be guided towards things that you still need to heal from, but this is all a beautiful unfoldment so you can come home to yourself. Journal to get more clarity on what it is you want, adding to it each time you get an intuitive download. The more specific it is and the more it feels right, the more it is likely to happen.

Exercise

Find a quiet space and with eyes closed, and really think about what you want. Is it still the same as when you first imagined your dream life? Add in as much detail as possible, including what you are doing for fun. What do your finances look like? What does your family setup look like? Do you travel? How old are you? Marinate in those lovely feelings you want to create. Now write down anything extra you saw. Just let it flow onto the paper as it comes. Expect to write two to three pages of what this looks like to you now. Now ask if this is what you really want. Close your eyes for a moment and ask again, with feeling, are these tangible dreams? Is this what you want?

Remember, a lot of this work is the gradual discovery of who you are. Today you might want to abseil down a large cliff or learn to ride a horse, but tomorrow you might want to sign up for a ten-hour course to brush up on your Photoshop skills. It's okay; this is your journey and nobody else's. We are here to have the full experience of life, and making heart-centred decisions *and* mistakes along the way is all part of gently taking you back to your true path. Your dream life statement is an evolving document—ever-changing and offering you options, ideas, opportunities, and experiences that you continually challenge, to decide whether it's really what you want. Keep asking, keep experiencing, keep going within. It's okay if you keep changing your mind.

Focus

"What you choose to focus on becomes your reality."

—Jen Sincero

Be deliberate about where you focus your energy and attention. You want to manifest your most awesome life? Put your attention, intention, and focus on what you want and be open to receiving it. When you don't focus on what you don't want, this disappears from your life. Instead of saying, "I don't want to be single", say, "I am in a loving relationship". Instead of saying, "I never have enough time and money", say, "I always have plenty of time, and money always flows to me". *Accomplishment comes from focusing on what you are doing.* When your mind wanders and you're not fully focused on what you want to achieve, this tells your subconscious that what you are doing doesn't deserve your full attention and you are likely to have poor judgment and miss opportunities. Train your brain to really focus on one thing at a time. Even if it's for a short period, like five or ten minutes. The more you do this, the more you will protect your ability to focus.

Trust and Surrender

"As far as I can tell, it's just about letting the universe know what you want and then working towards it while letting go of how it comes to pass."

—Jim Carrey

When you set expectations that things have to be or look a certain way, this is you trying to control the outcome. You're grinding out what you want within the confines of what you believe is available to you, so it's impossible to create your dreams. When you drop the expectation of how it has to look and open yourself to receiving it in the way that is right for you, that's when life becomes easy and effortless. You will pivot between the different stages of awakening in your life as you walk your path, accept this as all part of the process.

Have that resolute feeling of trust, knowing in your heart that the universe operates from a vibration of love so you can release and surrender, even when it's hard. Allow life to take you in all directions and don't fear failure. There is *no such thing* as failure, it is just an experience for you to learn from. Don't ignore the energy pulling you in new directions. When you ignore it, you fall out of alignment, and that's when the uncomfortable feelings come through again and you feel life is out of your control. When you trust that everything always works out for your own good, it's incredible and liberating. You're no longer forcing a situation, you're calibrating up to that next version of you and surrendering to something far bigger: a force with only your best interests at heart. The more you embody your soul, the more you create what you want. Don't get frustrated—the universe doesn't work on time, it works on trust and alignment.

Connecting to Nature

Everything in nature is created from the same space as source, God, and the universe—that same high-vibe frequency as love. As Shakti Gawain says, "One of the major ways we are out of alignment with our souls is our disconnect from nature. We have kind of lost our natural way of being connected to the planet. We need to be rooted on the planet. We experience ourselves as being isolated from that and I actually think that that is a great cause of the suffering many of us are experiencing, consciously or subconsciously."

How can you bring more nature into your life so you feel more connected to those high-frequency vibrations? How can you get outside, away from the hustle, bustle, and noise of modern life? The options are endless. Being in nature allows you to experience the awe of the world, the abundance of life around us, the beauty and pure perfection of what the universe creates. Grounding meditations are especially helpful. They root us into the earth and keep us connected to the universe. Doing them outside is even better. You can also ground yourself by walking barefoot outside on the natural earth to allow the negative ions to feed into your body which neutralises our "charge", delivering numerous health benefits *and* positively affecting our emotions.

12

Envisioning Your Perfect Life

"Everything you imagine is real."

— Pablo Picasso

Now that you accept that creating your magnificent life is based on pure conscious awareness, you have discovered how to proactively call what you want into your life with ease. As you heal, you can step into your power by using the alchemy and healing from lack and scarcity and start telling yourself a powerful new story. This is you convincing your brain of new beliefs, thoughts, and feelings, a magical place as if you already have what you want.

"Imagination is everything.
It is the preview of life's coming attraction."

— Albert Einstein

By far, the most powerful way to tell your brain a new story is through visualisation. Focusing on what you want and evoking the emotion as if you already have it tricks the brain into thinking this is real. Your brain cannot differentiate between reality and fantasy. This is why we did so much work to discover who you really are and align what you want with the desires of your soul.

The Background to Visualisation

Visualisation techniques (along with meditation and gratitude practices) have been used for centuries to help prepare the mind (and body) to create a desired reality. Think about it: it's the "visionaries" that have changed the world. World-class athletes, CEOs, and entrepreneurs all use the powers of visualisation to help them get what they want. Think of everything that has been invented. It all started with a powerful thought, and then a vision, before becoming real. Everything that's been created was the result of someone's initial vision.

The Australian psychologist Alan Richardson set out to prove that visualisation works, using an experiment that involved basketball players. He divided the players into three groups. The first group practised twenty minutes of free throws a day. The second group visualised themselves making free throws perfectly but didn't physically practice. The third group did neither. The results showed that the second group showed a significant improvement in their free-throwing skills and were almost as accurate as the ones that practised. The third group regressed in their skills. This shows that visualisation can be a powerful tool, which is why it is such a well-known technique among athletes.

"Visualization—or the act of creating compelling and vivid pictures in your mind—may be the most underutilised success tool you possess because it greatly accelerates the achievement of any success."

—Jack Canfield

Most humans don't use their imagination proactively or constructively. Most use it destructively, letting the subconscious tell them negative thoughts. When you use your imagination powerfully, it is the perfect tool to create what you want. You're *thinking into being,* believing and acting, as if you've already gotten what you want. This is you, telling yourself new stories, with new patterns of thoughts. You're fine-tuning the future version of yourself. When you step into this place, the more you're connected with your spirit, the more inspired and limitless you will become.

What Is Visualisation?

Visualisation is the act of intentionally and deliberately seeing what you want before you have it. It is the *focused mental recreation of thoughts, images, sounds, and environments* that prime the brain to believe what you want is already happening. By visualising what you want, your brain will get to work on creating it because it always wants to prove itself right. Your brain learns by repetition, just like when you are studying for an exam. You keep re-reading and revising the same module until you know it. The same goes for getting what you want. Visualisation is one of the most powerful skills humans have, but most of the world hasn't been taught that we have this incredible superpower.

You don't have to look very far to get examples of famous people who use the power of visualisation. Jim Carrey (actor, writer, and producer) openly speaks about how powerful visualisation is. He is known to have carried around a "dream cheque" he made out to himself to the sum of ten million dollars for "acting services rendered" when he was a poor struggling actor. He kept this cheque in his wallet to keep himself inspired and focused and would often hold it and feel as if he had received it already. He then went on to earn that exact amount for his role in *Dumb and Dumber* in 1994. Carrey credits daily visualisation to help get him there.

Look at people like Oprah Winfrey—the multi-millionaire media mogul who came from complete poverty. Every day as a child, watching her grandmother, she would affirm to herself, "My life won't be like this. My life won't be like this. It will be better." She talks about the award-winning film *The Color Purple*, released in 1985 and based on a book that she was absolutely obsessed with. She says she ate, slept, and thought about *The Color Purple* continuously, wanting to act in the screenplay. One day, whilst on a retreat to help her lose her much-publicised weight, she received the call for a movie. That audition was for *The Color Purple*. Although it hadn't manifested initially (she had been called for a different movie and was disappointed it wasn't it), when she let go of how it had to look and surrendered to a much bigger power, the call from Steven Spielberg then came through to say she had the part. She says she had literally drawn the film into her life from the power of her thoughts and visualisation. "The way you think creates the reality for yourself. You can change your reality based on the way you think," says Winfrey. "Create the highest, grandest vision possible for your life because you become what you believe."

Lady Gaga, the American singer and songwriter, says, "I knew I was famous before anyone even knew me." She thought, felt, and acted like all those she'd admired before she become world-renowned. She had a mantra she would repeat every day: "Music is my life. Music is my life. The fame is inside of me. I'm going to make a number-one record with number-one hits. And if it is not yet, it's a lie." As she says, "You're saying a lie over and over and over again, and then one day, the lie is true. You have to have a deep sense of conviction and confidence in your abilities and have that feeling in every fibre of your being. You have to have a deep sense of your own greatness and your own ability from a very deep place inside of you." It is this that drives you to create the reality you want.

"The imagination is the most marvellous, miraculous, inconceivable powerful force the world has ever known."

— Napoleon Hill

Creative visualisation is the focused effort of forming images in your mind, training your brain for what you want versus letting it wander. When you visualise, you are sending out a clear signal to the universe and attracting the same back, helping you create your abundant life.

For creative visualisation to be effective, you need to believe what you want is available. Sometimes those dreams seem so far away, but they're not. For your amazing future to be created, you need to have big visualisations. Give yourself permission to *see and think big*. There is no ceiling; the only limitation is your mind. If you can see it, you can achieve it.

The Science Behind Visualisation

"Imagination is more important than knowledge."

— Albert Einstein

When you imagine something, the knowledge that says you can't do that doesn't exist. Imagination is more powerful than logic or knowledge. The subconscious runs on fantasies and delusions of negativity, so visualisation has the power to harness this by proactively choosing fantasies of what you want. As Jack Canfield says, "If you can hold it in your mind, you can hold it in your hand." When you direct energy from your thoughts and emotions, you create what you want, because where attention goes, energy flows.

Our brains are constantly gathering and filtering information and steering our behaviours based on our thoughts, emotions, and beliefs. They are continually making new connections and pruning off old ones. Therefore, if our thought processes are constantly changing as we experience and adapt to our physical environments, we then can influence this with what we think, experience, and feel. If we apply conscious awareness using the power of our thoughts and add in the power of visualisation, we have the capacity to make our brains believe anything. You're installing a new programme. The more you do this, the stronger the connections between the cells, and this becomes your new way of thinking. Brain rewiring cannot be done overnight, it starts with training your brain each day using the power of your thoughts and visualisation.

"Visualization facilitates manifestation so when you imagine it has to happen, you create a situation for it to happen."

—Joe Dispenza

According to Joe Dispenza, one hour of focused concentration doubles the number of connections in the brain. You must review it with concentrated thinking about what you want; otherwise, the circuits will fall away. You do this by visualising and feeling what you want. When you apply your new thinking, this affects your behaviour. *This is you, acting like you have what you want.* This is a constant process—a way of life. But by doing it repeatedly, you override the default setting of your original thoughts and upgrade the internal software, creating a new future and taking it into your own hands. This means you have to think, act, feel, and believe as if you're already doing it. *You're walking in the energy frequency of your future.* As Dispenza says, "By creating a vision so clear and real, those thoughts become 'the experience' so the brain's synapses begin to wire that information *as if it were reality.* If you can get your behaviour to match your intentions, your actions to match your thoughts, get your mind and body to work together you'll have a new experience (of your reality)." You have the power to create your reality by clearly visualising what you want. Focus on bringing out all the details until you create that a new level of vibration. Then you're acting in alignment, with absolute conviction, so you can trust that it will manifest with ease instead of effort.

Dispenza continues, "It is going to be uncomfortable; you are going to have to make different choices. You will have to start doing different things. There's uncertainty, and you can't predict it." The brain hates this change and unfamiliarity. As soon as you feel that familiar fear, regret, or hopelessness, you know that you are back in the energy and emotions of the past. He goes on to say, "If the body is conditioned to predictability, then your brain is going to really hate your visualisation." You will be tempted to go back to the familiar comfort zone of automatic thinking where you end up creating the same future as your past, which is why we don't think we have the power to change our lives.

Visualisation Techniques

Cognitive Priming

This is you "priming your brain" with that new different experience you want.

John Assaraf, mindset and behaviour expert, calls this "mental rehearsal" as a visualisation technique to create what you want.

Exercise

Go back to your dream life statement and read through it. Find a quiet space and sit with your eyes closed. Turn on some meditation music if you like and start to imagine that you already have what you want. Envision it, adding all your senses. When you think about it, does it evoke excitement and joy? Is it from your heart? Is the intention behind it pure? Are you feeling those incredible, high-vibe emotions of love, peace, and freedom? When you do this, creative thinking is building a vision in your mind. It doesn't matter how much money you have or why you believe you can't have it or how much help you have. Visualise what you want and revel in it.

Say how much you love it. Your brain responds to all of this. Feel this energy and breathe it in.

I do this for five to ten minutes in the morning and at night before bed. I consciously work through the different life domains one by one: relationships, money, career, well-being, and so on. I marinate in how wonderful it feels to already have it. When I visualise what I want, I physically feel the frisson of energy racing around my body.

Vision Boarding

A vision board is a physical representation of your dreams, desires, goals, inspiration, and aspirations for your life using pictures. It is a powerful visualisation tool because when you look at it, your brain is extremely focused. It works by helping to filter through the information that is available to our brains, so it just focuses on the things you want. The more you focus on this, the more you will manifest it into your reality.

John Assaraf is a firm believer in the power of vision boards. In 1995, he created a vision board and put it somewhere he would see daily: his home office. Whenever he thought about or saw something he wanted, he would find a picture and add it to the board. Most importantly, he would see himself acting as if he already had what he desired. Five years later, after moving house, his son discovered the old vision boards, which had been in storage. They contained pictures of various things, such as a car and a watch—all of which he had acquired by then. When he looked at the next vision board, he began to cry, for on that board was a picture of the house he had just bought and was living in! It was the very house he had cut out of a home magazine four years earlier.

I love my vision board. It is extremely motivational and a powerful technique to get what you want. I credit my vision board for helping me create the money I've received, the exact house in nature I wanted, my home office, my health goals, my family's happiness, our travel and adventures, my business, and this book!

Why Vision Boards Are So Effective

Vision boarding is more impactful than just having a "goal" or to-do list (which itself is more impactful than not having it written down at all) because pictures are more remembered than words. This is called the Pictorial Superiority Effect.[18][19] According to Allan Paivio's "Dual Coding Theory", pictures have advantages over words in how they are coded and retrieved in the stored memory of the brain. Images are coded more easily whilst words require a dual coding process so are more difficult to recall in the brain.[20]

In the brain, there is a network of neurons called the reticular activating system (RAS) which help to filter the millions and millions of bits of information we are inundated with every day. We cannot possibly process all of these—we would explode. The RAS spends all day filtering through your life and will only find evidence to confirm what you believe. Combined with the Pictorial Superiority Effect, using images and pictures over words can powerfully "imprint" your brain to believe the new story you're telling yourself. The brain *cannot* differentiate between fantasy and reality; imagination will always defy logic and reasoning in the brain. *This* is what translates to your visualisation superpowers.

---

18 Snodgrass, J.G., Asiaghi, A. The pictorial superiority effect in recognition memory. *Bull. Psychon. Soc.* **10,** 1–4 (1977). https://doi.org/10.3758/BF03333530

19 Whitehouse, Andrew JO, Murray T. Maybery, and Kevin Durkin. "The development of the picture superiority effect." *British Journal of Developmental Psychology* 24.4 (2006): 767-773.

20 Paivio, A., Csapo, K. Short-term sequential memory for pictures and words. *Psychon Sci* **24,** 50–51 (1971). https://doi.org/10.3758/BF03337887

You can make vision boards for anything, in any domain of your life. Using pictures cut from magazines or downloaded, you can place these on a big piece of A2 cardboard, some notice board, a journal, or a book. There are whole books dedicated to vision boarding, and there isn't a right or wrong way to do it.

When you make your board, keep asking what areas of your life are the most important to you. Are your current actions in alignment with your values and what you truly want? Add words that resonate with you, such as success, prosperity, love, gratitude, worthy, happy, or healthy. I often add a photo of myself in the middle and position the pictures in sections, so the brain is very guided. The fulfilment and beauty that comes from making your board will fill you up with excitement and enthusiasm of what you want *is* possible.

Making vision boards feels good because it is a creative process that releases the brain's feel-good hormones, such as serotonin and oxytocin. It is contemplative, tactile, visual, emotional, and motivational. It's an amazing exercise for self-awareness and self-reflection. It's important to be guided by your intuition and not be too cognitive in the process as you do this. It's more about being in an intuitive space that helps you listen within for what you really want and be aware of the emotional state attached to it.

Put your board in a place where you can see it as much as possible. Spend at least ten minutes looking at your board every day, floating in the bliss of your dreams. If you are aligned with who you are and what you want, it will feel magical and exciting. This seeps into your subconscious, so eventually your conscious brain will catch up and you will start to behave in ways that bring it in.

There's a running joke with my clients about the power of vision boards and being extremely attentive to what goes on there because it tends to come true. One of my clients added her dream career to her vision board, along with the salary she wanted and even a picture of a horse. It was her dream to work with horses. She spent much of her childhood surrounded by them, as her dad was a jockey. She looked at it every day. In the span of three months, she created that job (with the job title she had written), the identical salary, and the company was located right next to stables and paddocks. She couldn't believe what she had created!

Creating a vision board causes so much transformation—you've started to own the process of getting what it is you want. It's like a wave of relief washing over you, getting all your dreams and desires onto a board. Whilst it is suggested to focus on what you want to achieve in one year (although as Assaraf shows, longer-term visions are also possible, given the house he manifested), you can add longer-term goals on there. You can also add or remove pictures and words over time. Keep your vision boards or take a picture and save it on your computer.

Now you're entering a beautiful place, armed with the skills, techniques, processes, and science-backed evidence, so you can really envision with unwavering faith you can create what you want.

PART 3

ABUNDANCE

13

Creating The Overflow

"Making a dream into reality begins with what you have, not with what you are waiting on."

— T F Hodge

Welcome to the final part of your unfoldment: understanding that everything you want is available to you *right now*. When you open yourself up to receiving everything that is available to you, you start living the life you desire and experiencing those feelings of freedom. The power to create all you want is *already inside of you*. It's just your conditioned mindset and negative automatic thinking that's getting in the way. When you truly embrace abundance, you are creating your own reality—a place of overflow where all your needs are met.

What Is Abundance?

Most people think abundance is having a lot of money and wealth because the western world is geared towards the importance of materialistic things and the importance of money. Think about it. When you meet someone for the first time, the first question asked is often "what do you do?" or "where do you live?" as opposed to the more telling questions of "who are you?" or "what do you love to do?" Even though "wealth" is associated with financial prosperity, it actually refers to a state of mind. It has its origins in the Middle

English word *wele* meaning well-being, happiness, and prosperity in abundance.

Therefore, abundance is so much more than just financial wealth. Simply put, it means having a lot in *any* area of your life. This could mean love, intelligence, wisdom, health, beauty, time, success, happiness, peace, or confidence, as well as a financial attachment. It's about creating the overflow and feeling *prosperous* in all the areas in which you want to feel fulfilled. It's about being able to ask and receive *everything you need,* and having the deep respect and understanding that life *is* limitless.

Exercise

What would your life look like, feel like, and be like if you had unshakable self-belief and the determination to create anything you wanted? If your mind worked *for you* and wasn't diminished by self-imposed beliefs, so you can do anything and take responsibility for what you want with dedication and commitment? Sit in it. Doesn't that feel incredible?

You Were Born Abundant

When we live in victimhood, we don't believe that what we want is available to us. We live with a mentality of *scarcity*—not rich enough, not powerful enough, thin enough, relevant enough, perfect enough, not enough sleep, not enough time, not enough patience. We repeatedly hear stories about how we are unable to have what we want, so we close ourselves down and stop the overflow of this into our lives. When my children were younger, they always asked for things in abundance —ponies, castles, more toys, more holidays, candy, screen time, cars, and so on. An unconscious lack response would be, "Who do you think you are to want all that?"

This would be followed by guilt for seemingly saying no all the time. This used to trigger me and make me feel outraged that nothing was enough. Little did I know that these throwaway comments and berating of their innocently abundant attitude closed down their incredible limitless mindset. Slowly but surely, that divine overflow mindset is replaced with programming. If we do feel abundant, it feels so unnatural and uncomfortable that we subconsciously push it away. We create overwhelming situations of stress or feeling rushed because we are used to not having enough time. If we have unbridled happiness with a partner or family members, it might feel so unfamiliar that we create arguments or difficult situations to bring us back down to the level at which we feel more comfortable, even if it's miserable.

Think about it. Do you only find beauty when you put on your make-up or go on a hectic crash diet? What about success? When you feel accomplished, do you feel so out of your comfort zone you dismiss the compliments and bring yourself back down. What about money? When you receive a bonus or a monetary gift does this feel so uncomfortable you spend it almost as fast as you received it?

Unless you were fortunate enough to be brought up with highly conscious parents, or with a prosperous background, this block on abundance will be the driving factor of how you live your life. It will get in the way of basking in the overflow that is divinely yours for the taking. As Wayne Dyer says, "Everything you're currently against (e.g., your fears and self-limiting beliefs) are blocking you from abundance."

I'm not dismissing the outliers of the world here. There is a huge number of people who have come from nothing and gone on to show us that it is possible to have it all. Singers, actors, and other famous people are great examples of this. Our brains are hardwired that life is a *struggle* and what we want isn't available. So, what is it the outliers have that you don't? It's that abundant mindset, the absolute belief that anything is possible, that the universe is full of potential. It's just false perception stopping you from becoming the awesome individual you are. When you wake up and recognise it's all an illusion, you'll see it's all available to you.

Exercise

Try this Louise Hay exercise on prosperity. Close your eyes and imagine you are standing in front of the ocean, holding a container. Look at it. Is it a small, cracked mug, a huge jar, a bucket, or a massive tub? What are you taking from the ocean of life? However much we take, that ocean will *never* run dry. There is always enough. That container you hold is your *consciousness*, what you choose to believe is available. This is all to do with what you believe you are worthy of (being able to ask) and what you think you deserve (being able to receive). When you don't have what you want, it's because you aren't allowing yourself to accept that everything is within reach. Life isn't against us, life works for us and it's here to support us in every way possible.

What Are Your Beliefs About Abundance?

Look back at your life domains and consider how you feel about what you are worthy and deserving of in these areas.

Do you think you're worthy of abundance?

Do you think it's selfish to have everything you want?

Do you think you can have anything you want?

Do you think if you have more, others will have less?

Is it safe to feel abundant?

Wouldn't it be incredible to live in the state of the overflow? Not dimming your light, but living in alignment with who you are, stepping into your power turning up that light until you shine like the star you are. A vision of having it all, living in that space of bliss and freedom so you're vibrating at your highest frequency. Wouldn't that feel incredible?

> ***"The journey to (financial) freedom starts the minute you decide you were destined for prosperity, not scarcity—for abundance, not lack. Isn't there a part of you that has always known that? Can you see yourself living a bounteous life—a life of more than enough? It only takes one minute to decide. Decide now."***
>
> ***— Mark Victor Hansen***

The key to living an abundant life is knowing that everything comes from inside you—this divine spiritual place of your soul—and trusting what feels right for you. It's you choosing to live consciously from that place. Within it, the power of infinite creativity is just waiting for you to use it. Whether you desire more love, more money, better health, or success, this is all yours to accept, once you stop resisting it. When you dare to relinquish the belief that you don't deserve it or it's unavailable to you, you can attract anything you want in life. To gain true abundance, remember who you are: rich, divine, limitless, incredible, and ever-growing.

You are enough, just by being born. When you start embodying it, living as if you already have what you want, you start vibrating at "enough". Abundance will flow to you, there can be no other way. The universe is always expanding. Abundance is never depleted, it is everywhere, so recognise prosperity and wholeness in all the areas of your life.

Exercise

Where is there abundance in your life right now?

How will you know when you have abundance in your life?

Cultivating Abundance

You need to be okay with feeling like you deserve what you want. Otherwise, you will block it. Does it feel okay to ask for and receive immense wealth? Barely fifty years ago, women weren't allowed to have independent financial wealth! The patriarchal system the world has been set up as means there is deep programming amongst women that not only keeps us from feeling like we deserve it, but doesn't even let us believe we can ask for it! Also, the class system throughout the world means people have been programmed to believe it's not okay to ask for or receive. Remember, a vast majority of us haven't even been told how to create wealth! The top one percent of those with immense wealth have zero coding around whether they can have it or not; they just get on with it. Receiving is an art; you need to become accustomed and open to it. If not, it will stop you from getting what you want and keep you in a place of lack. You cannot create what you want unless you embody the absolute riches that the universe has bestowed on you. It is not possible to create the physical manifestation of what you desire when you are emotionally and energetically repelling it!

As Louise Hay says, if you view invoices as "enemies", you will never have enough. Ultimately, a bill means someone has trusted you enough to provide a service or product. It feels good to contribute and circulate money—paying that invoice or spending money in a shop gives someone a job so they can then go on and circulate money.

The abundance that is available to us is enormous. There is an overflow of food, money, time, happiness if we choose to see it. Yes, it is true there are a lot of people with little, but *abundance goes where it is desired, not needed.* Hay continues, "Feeling lonely is nothing to do with unavailable relationships, it's because we fear being rejected or being abandoned." So we put up walls and push people away and don't let them in.

Think about the abundance of air and water. According to National Geographic, only 1.2 percent of the world's water is drinkable, but have we ever run out? No! Rivers and streams keep running and the water cycle keeps on happening. We've even invented desalination plants and created reservoirs, so we always have water. The abundance of trees and flora on our planet gives us the oxygen we need. Do you ever run out of air? No, of course you don't. We all breathe and drink, we just assume there is enough and take it for granted. So how can you imprint this abundant belief into every area of your life?

True abundance starts with a thought, then the deliberate intention to have a clear understanding of what you want. It requires awareness, intention, and listening within. Ask what you would like to have more in your life, how would that feel if you created an overflow of what you wanted? Keep asking. Plant the seed of your intention and allow the universe to take care of the details. Your brain listens to you constantly, so tell yourself new stories. You have the motivation and desire to live your best life, to really believe in yourself. This mindset seeps into all areas of your life to create abundance. As Marisa Peer tell us to say "I believe it because I can see it" instead of "I won't believe it until I see it".

To think abundantly, you must recognise that growth is necessary, so you must take risks and expand outside of your comfort zone. Choose to live in the zone of unlimited potential! You can't expand or be open to receiving everything you want whilst you have a fixed mindset. This will just keep you stuck. If you believe you already know everything, you will severely limit your learning and growth. In abundance, there is a never-ending thirst for knowledge and to develop new skills. Those with an abundant mindset see limitless possibilities in the world, and focus on what's working instead of what isn't.

You *are* deserving and worthy. Life is an adventure of unlimited possibilities. Those that think abundantly are present, conscious, confident, determined, and deliberate with their intentions. Abundance means you are optimistic and joyful. You accept the curveballs and change as part of this human life experience. When you think abundantly, you control your environment, *not* the other way round. You intentionally plan the future and have a vision so clear and defined that you're already living as your future self.

Believe in yourself and your personal power. Laugh at your self-limiting beliefs and forgive yourself for carting them around like a heavy backpack. When you believe in yourself and grow confidence in your abilities and personal power, you can accomplish *anything*!

Exercise

A great exercise to start thinking abundantly at the beginning of the day is to think of something small that you want to bring into your life—a colour, a number, a word. Keep it at the forefront of your mind and pay close attention to all the ways the universe brings it in your life. At the end of the day, reflect on all the ways that colour, number, or word came into your experience. Whilst this is a simple exercise, you will understand the power you have to manifest when you direct your energy and intention to them.

Role-Playing

A really great way of drawing in and creating that abundant feeling is to think about someone (real or imagined, dead or alive) that strikes you as having the abundance you want. It can be anyone, if you truly admire them. Many of my corporate, highly cognitive clients tend to think of people such as Richard Branson, Jeff Bezos, Elon Musk, Warren Buffet, or Michelle Obama. My more esoteric or ethereal ones think of people such as the Dalai Lama, Brené Brown, Oprah Winfrey, or Deepak Chopra. Me? I tend to live in a world that looks like a mixture of these people and how they think, feel, act, and believe. I think about how their beliefs became truths with absolute determination and focus. Your role models can be a mixture of different people too. Just someone you really want to emulate and embody. If you think about the mindset of that person, their beliefs, and their actions, you can bring them into being. Read their stories, watch them on screen. Tell yourself that's *your* story, that's *you* doing what they do. Your role is to become them, just like an actor. Pay close attention to the energy you feel in those moments. Keep it at the forefront of your mind and notice how you begin to view yourself and how others treat you. Is that beginning to create abundance in what you desire?

Gratitude and Abundance

"Be thankful for what you have; you'll end up having more. If you concentrate on what you don't have, you will never, ever have enough."

— Oprah Winfrey

When you practice gratitude—and I mean sincerely practice it—it is one of the strongest and most transformative methods of bringing abundance into your life. It shifts your perspective from lack and scarcity to having it all, where all your needs are met. This allows you to focus on the good in your life, which in turn pulls more goodness into your reality.

Every time I pay for a coffee, I say "thank you", not just to the cashier, but in my heart I also thank the barista who made my drink, the inventors of the espresso machine, the discovery of the coffee plant and whoever thought to turn it into a drink as well as the owner of the restaurant. Once you start, it is impossible not to feel gratitude for the abundance that surrounds you.

Get Into Nature

Nature is the best example of true abundance. There is an infinite amount of air, sunlight, grass, grains of sand, leaves on the trees, and more. Spend time in nature; really breathe it in. Remind yourself just how incredible and miraculous the world is. Look at the beauty and intricacies of the flora and fauna that surrounds you. The energy that nature gives off is that same high-vibrational frequency as source, as love. When you think of a flower, that tiny seed has everything it needs to become the incredible bloom it will be one day. That apple seed? It has the potential to create an entire apple tree with an abundance of fruit. Think of how the animal kingdom has everything inside it already, even before new life is created. This includes you. Inside, you have everything you need to create what you want. When a woman is born, she has up to one million unfertilised eggs in her, ready to create life. It only takes one egg and one sperm cell (from millions) to create the miracle that is life. Doesn't that completely blow your mind? When you sit in that place and truly be thankful for the phenomenon that is you, it has the capacity to take you to that place of abundance.

Meditate on Abundance

This is a unique opportunity to connect to the source from which all abundance flows: your inner quiet. Your spiritual, divine being. Let go of all thoughts, observe the inflow and outflow of your breath, and start relaxing with each. You can use a guided meditation or practise a mantra, such as:

- I am open to receiving gifts from the universe
- I am abundant
- The river of abundance flows towards me

- I am wealthy
- I am always attracting abundance
- I am happy and full of joy.
- The core of my being is the ultimate reality
- I behold the abundance which surrounds my life

Releasing Guilt and Practising Forgiveness

"If you feel guilt, your mind will become a judge, a jury, and a jailor."

— Marisa Peer

True abundance does not have room for guilt. The only benefit of guilt is knowing you've done something wrong and that you wouldn't do it again. When we feel guilt and shame, we punish ourselves and self-sabotage because we don't feel worthy or deserving of having what we want. It is totally self-destructive because it prevents you from reaching your amazing potential and creating the abundance you *are* deserving of.

Forgive yourself for every mistake you've ever made, and you'll become free of the need to sabotage yourself. We learn and evolve as humans by making mistakes, and it is this which lets us find our way back onto our paths. How many times did you fall over as a baby learning to walk? How many incorrect answers did you give in math as you were learning to count? If you don't forgive yourself, your mind will keep you stuck.

Make a List

Deepak Chopra suggests making a list of fifty people who have influenced your life. They can be alive, departed, family members, friends, people in the public domain. Anyone who has contributed to your development and growth. When you're making this list, really think about why you chose this person and how that changed your life for the better. Move calmly and thoughtfully; it might take time to get to those fifty people. More will pop into your mind as you think your way through this. This exercise demonstrates the ease, flow, and abundance of people that have easily come into your life, affecting it in a positive way.

Be Present

"The fastest way to bring more wonderful examples of abundance into your personal experience is to take constant notice of the wonderful things that are already there."

— Esther Hicks

Live with the mental lens of abundance. Be extremely present and open to what is already around you. Each day, set an abundant intention of how you want to feel. Put reminders on your phone or notes on your fridge to remind you of your intention. Abundant intentions might include choosing to think abundantly, catching yourself when you think of lack, or basking in the abundance that surrounds you.

Life is short, so live large and believe in the endless possibilities life has to offer. Choose to live an abundant life, creating memories you will cherish forever. Be open and receptive to all the good that is around you.

Releasing Resistance and Accepting Change

"Abundance comes in many forms, do not limit your abundance by trying to control how it will flow, just know that it will come."

— Shelly Sullivan

Letting go of how things must look is a huge step towards becoming abundant. As is trusting that everything you want is on its way. When you try to control how your world looks, that's operating from fear instead of trusting your soul. Don't give in to your subconscious fear of the unknown. As you move towards an abundant mindset, be conscious of those uncomfortable feelings. Remind yourself that predictable lives will never create magnificent lives.

14

Stepping Into Your Power (And Why You Don't Want To)

"Whatever makes you uncomfortable is your biggest opportunity for growth."

— Bryant M McGill

Personal development takes a willingness to change, commitment, motivation, and a *deep-seated belief that anything you want is possible*. It takes acceptance and the bravery to choose to go within and do the work to uncover who you really are in your soul, even when it's painful. It takes courage to recognise what you need to heal from and where you need to forgive, but courage comes from the heart. You will stumble. You will make mistakes and fall off your path along the way. Let's be honest: the easier way out is not to bother. But if you don't, you will stay stuck. Like the seed of a flower, you have everything to flourish and show your beauty to the world inside you already. You just have to allow it to unfold. It's hard to keep a level head with your blinkers on, striving towards your highest potential whilst everyone else is losing theirs. It's too easy to relent and slip back into collective consciousness belief patterns. Don't be scared of being afraid, it's only fear of the unknown. Feel it, and choose to do it anyway.

When you feel any fear or the pain of procrastination bubbling up, pause, take a breath, bring yourself back to your truth, stay present, and listen to your energy. Remind yourself *why* you are doing it because that becomes the high-performance fuel for the inner engine of your soul. Trust in the process of your transformation. If you're prepared to peel back the layers, you are absolutely on your way to greatness. Release those you blamed and shamed, choosing instead to process those emotions so you move on. You will oscillate back and forth between different stages of your awakening. Look at the different domains of your life and see where you've grown and what needs attention.

It's easy to slip into negative thinking: "Why am I doing all this work when most of the world doesn't?" But your job is to evolve—to live consciously and authentically. *That is all the universe or God wants for you.* If everyone else wants to come to your high-vibe, authentically aligned party, that's great—it's an open invite. You're doing this work so *you* can evolve, so *you* can experience your life in its greatness. It is no one else's life to live, it is *yours*. Do not lose sight of this.

Change and Resistance

Your conscious development can make you feel unstoppable as you take back what is rightfully yours, attacking the world in full force. On the other hand, it can feel scary and totally out of your comfort zone. Whilst we might consciously desire something different, our resistance may be strong because of our subconscious desire to keep ourselves safe. Those nagging thoughts drift in, suggesting it might be impossible, silly, deluded, unacceptable, or unachievable. We fear change and failure and might also feel angry at recognising a need to change when others just carry on obliviously. The recognition of this resistance is a *good* thing. It is all part of your healing! Celebrate this! Any reaction you have at your evolution is to be welcomed, as it shows you are open to healing, transformation, and reclaiming what is rightfully yours.

The Blocks in Your Path to Change

"Change is never painful.
Only the resistance to change is painful."

— Buddha

That initial desire to change from the heart is often met with resistance in the mind. This is perfectly normal. We have an inbuilt fear of change—we fear failing, being rejected, or what others may think. You might even fear your success. Maybe you worry you'll hurt others by saying no and focusing on what you want. All resistance does it keep you frustrated and in a place where you feel disempowered and unhappy, becoming resentful as you bury your true feelings. It's too easy to fall back into old stories of *not being enough*, but that's how we give our power away and then use it as an excuse to never change. You've operated so long in a certain way, it's too easy to slip back into it. You're addicted to the struggle. It's your emotional home, a place of familiarity and safety, even if you're unhappy. Be mindful of how you resist and get in the way of yourself. Be conscious of what you are choosing not to see.

The key to breaking this is awareness. You're attuned to this now, so anytime you get triggered and are tempted *to put yourself in the way*, recognise the trigger, stop, and remind yourself you have no business being drawn into the drama and the illusion of perception because *you no longer operate like this.* Break the pattern: say a prechosen word, pinch yourself, leave the room, dance, laugh, jump up and down, whatever action you can put in place to consciously stop yourself from going down the vortex. *Focus on where you want that energy to go to, instead of where you allow it to unconsciously flow.* Recognise the dissonance, even when you're low-vibe, and remind yourself *why* you're doing it. All those reasons above are easily overcome and part of life. Just keep going back to what drives you and the outcome of your dreams. Acknowledge the consequences of not making the change and striving towards your best life.

Tick off every day on a calendar as you inch towards the new version of you. Your brain will love it! Keep pushing through until those new thoughts, beliefs, and habits become your new emotional home.

Creating Your Personal Force Field

"Why is feeling safe, less than and undeserving of an amazing existence, better than one of living your truth and being the blessed, incredible human, you actually are?"

— Sara Longoria

You've got to set boundaries, so you put your needs and wants first. Remind yourself that it is safe to speak up for what you want. Failures or mistakes are all just lessons in life showing you what you want and guiding you gently back to your path. The only failure is to never try. Don't be swayed by others' judgement or criticism. You choose what you let in. Judgement and criticism are entirely based on perception and a projection of that individual's fears and unmet needs. It is the lowest form of knowledge, requiring no accountability, understanding, or foresight. Remind yourself that your life is divine and precious, and you have the absolute right to live it with peace, freedom, grace, and happiness. Do you want to look back with regret because of what someone said? Say, "I love you", in the mirror every day, and remind yourself of your greatness.

"Be not afraid of growing slowly; be afraid only of standing still."

— Chinese Proverb

You cannot eat the whole elephant in one go, so be gentle with yourself and accept that you are exactly where you need to be on your path. You need to recognise your achievements and remind yourself of what a powerful creator you are, so you keep on putting one foot in front of the other. *Be thankful for being shown what you do and don't want.* You love yourself so much that you're willing to allow yourself to live to your highest potential. You are worthy of the most incredible life, and the power to make this happen is already within you.

You didn't know what you were doing, but now you've woken up. Respect and use this power consciously for your benefit. We all have lessons to learn, and the universe will give you more to learn from. Observe yourself, be curious and watch how you resist going back to your comfort zone. Then smile and say to yourself, "No, I choose to live from my truth".

How We Change

As we walk down our path of authenticity, we often don't even truly recognise change. Many think growth doesn't happen until *total transformation* happens, but that is not true. The process begins when you first make the decision to change. In this case, it was picking up this book. Human beings want instant gratification; fast or not at all. But your beautiful growth is a step-by-step process, and it is meant to be revered with awe, love and appreciation, not cheapened by wanting it all immediately.

Change *can* happen instantly, but this is often driven by falling beneath those lowest "set points" (leaving an abusive relationship, bankruptcy, losing a house, death of a loved one). However, change is often insidious and not quite so obvious unless we become deliberately aware of our progress and recognise what we have achieved.

Model of Change

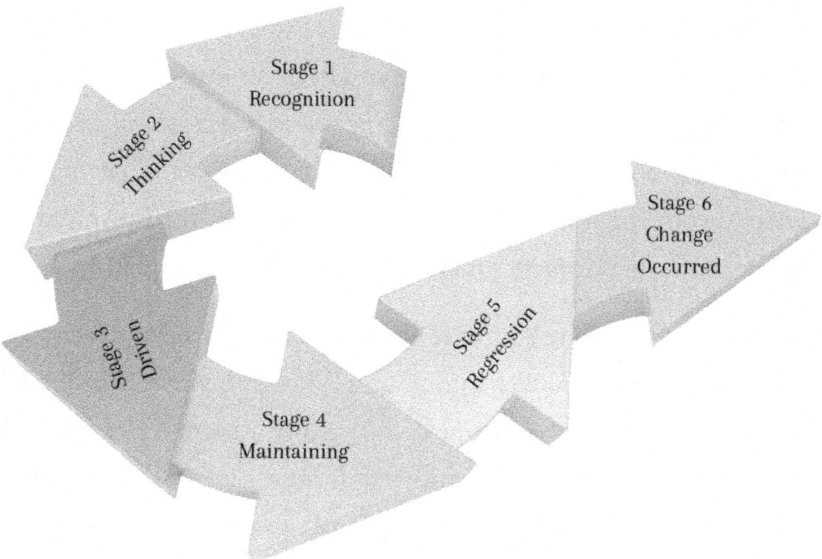

Model of Change Transformation

Stage 1: Recognising

You recognise you're unhappy with your current situation. You are listening to yourself, and you want something different. Enough is enough, and it's time to push through the upper "set point" barrier.

Stage 2: Thinking

You ruminate on how this problem has affected your life so far, how it is affecting you now, how it holds you back, and the reasons *why* you must change it. This is you either learning from pain ("I don't want this") or insight ("This would be a better way"). You feel empowered to make conscious decisions about how to move forward, including mindset work and action steps.

Stage 3: Driven

You take relevant action because you're feeling motivated. You're making headway by making small steps towards getting what you want. As Confucius said, "The man who moves mountains starts by moving small stones."

Stage 4: Action

This is where you are maintaining action; you're focusing on what you want and acting, feeling, and behaving as if it is happening. You visualise already having what you want, leaning into those incredible emotions you want to feel. This is you being discerning, driven, and excited at the potential that exists within you.

Stage 5: Regression

This is that "one step forward, two steps back" stage, where you behave in ways that sabotage your plans. *Recognise this regression and frustration.* This is a place of celebration! It's all part of the process. You need time for this new version of you to embed, at a cellular level. Lean into it—the unease, the dissonance. *It's only temporary.* Respect the lag time between where you are and where you want to be. Become the witness of your experience and love yourself through it.

Stage 6: Change

You've grown! Recognise it! Celebrate it! You're incredible! So often, we are only motivated by the next shiny thing, but you need to deliberately recognise what you've done, honour what you have achieved. You need to reflect and "reverse gap" by looking at where you were and where you are now. Acknowledge your growth and give yourself healthy doses of praise, love, and grace as you march on towards reaching the potential that you know exists within you.

Frustration

"To conquer frustration, one must be intensely focused on the outcome, not the obstacles."

— T F Hodge

It's easy to become despondent when you're not getting what you want from a self-imposed time scale. It's tempting to say, "See? I can't have what I want". All this does is create frustration, resentment, and fear.

When you're frustrated, you're being impatient instead of letting it come. This will keep you stuck in place because the universe will reflect this back to you. You lead, and the universe follows, saying yes to everything you think and believe. If you're feeling frustrated, that energy will attract more of that into your life. How you do anything is how you do everything, so if you're feeling frustrated at work, this energy will come through in your home life, friends, income, your kids, or your health goals.

"Nothing ever goes away until it has taught us what we need to learn."

— Pema Chödrön

You will get what you want when you have healed what needs to be healed. When you are aligned with your higher self and making decisions with pure intention—from love, not fear. See whatever comes up as a good thing. These are just rocks that you can navigate around in the stream of life.

If you want to experience true change, you need to recognise and release the energy of frustration, respect the process of unbecoming yourself, practise self-awareness and implement new thoughts and habits until *they* become your new neural patterns. You are undoing a lifetime of self-limiting beliefs and stories, so revere and respect this. Let the knowledge embed. Rest, accept, release it as you push through. It's all part of your evolution to becoming the version of who you were always meant to be. Bask in the knowledge that you've seen the light and *choose to live like your newly upgraded version 2.0.* Check in with yourself regularly. How are you showing up? Are you being the future version of you? Are you mindful of your thoughts and beliefs?

A Beautiful Exercise to Get into the I-Have-It-Already Space

Try this amazing exercise from Sara Longoria. First, recognise and marvel at the amazing being you actually are. Look at your accomplishments, values, and authentic self. Aren't you incredible and enough, just by being here? Go through each of them and remind yourself of your awesomeness, then practice gratitude.

For example:

- I built a business. I'm incredible. Thank you!
- I birthed three children. I created life! Thank you!
- I have overcome relationships that don't serve me. Thank you!
- I have mastered my health. Thank you!
- I have mastered gratitude. Thank you!
- I have mastered not worrying about money. Thank you!
- I have mastered not caring what others think. Thank you!

Allowing yourself to revel in this *makes you feel unstoppable*—because you really are! Now, think of all those things you want to create, and allow yourself to sit in the "I have it already" headspace. Bask in those feelings.

Then you start to *feel into the abundance* that is right within your grasp. This shifts the frustrated energy around what you want to the ultimate belief that it is possible. It feels incredible *and available.*

Then you start to get turned on by life, even when you're experiencing low-vibrational emotions. Choose to acknowledge and process those feelings. Say thank you to them for showing up and what still needs to be worked on. Even when you're not high vibe, you can still be excited about what's coming. Don't fear low vibrations. Practice loving acceptance and say, "Isn't this fantastic? What am I being shown right now? Is it true or just a story?" This is the next-level you. *You get to decide the future.*

Get Creative

> ***"Every child is an artist, the problem is staying an artist when you grow up."***
>
> ***— Pablo Picasso***

Being creative takes you away from the energy of being stuck and frustrated and puts you into the energy of being expansive. When you're in a creative flow, not only are you contributing to the expansion of the universe, but it also allows you to be open to ideas flowing to you—i.e., "inspired downloads" from the universe. Being creative is a form of self-expression. *We are born to create.* It allows you to feel free, with no judgement, in whatever outlet resonates best with you. Being creative builds confidence, so we are willing to take more risks and value ourselves more. It brings happiness and is meditative, helping to calm the brain, reducing stress and anxiety whilst you're in that contemplative flow. Choose to boost your creativity by being extremely aware of what you enjoy and how you can weave it into your life.

What Are Your Creative Talents?

My creative talents would be playing the piano, sewing, or painting—all of which I did as a child and have picked up again thirty years later. Feelings of pure joy and elation flood me when I play piano (often Lady Gaga), pretending to be on stage. Practice your creativity and incorporate them into your life. It's not just about being artistically creative. You can become more creative by mixing up your daily routine, different exercise activities, cooking different meals, changing your route to work, listening to music, or spending time in nature. The list is endless, so allow yourself to go there. It feels wonderful.

Time

Time is something that we allow to *bear down and manage us, constricting and contracting*. It has the capacity to stop us from fully expressing who we were always designed to be. Society values not having enough time. It is worn like a badge of honour. We confuse being busy with being needed.

However, time is just a made-up concept of the human world. It was created to give us structure, and a frame of reference in which to live our lives. It allows us to grow, succeed, and expand but also provides safety and familiarity. The problem is that this persistent illusion seeps into our fears, feeding into self-judgment and criticism when we feel we have not used time to the best of our abilities. We have a *lack mentality* towards it and are scared of running out. We are acutely aware that whilst we don't have control over time, *we do have control over how we use it*. It's our relationship with time we must address. If you think you don't have enough time or that you waste it, this is the energy you give off and you will create a reality where you keep attracting situations in which you don't have enough time. A life of feeling rushed, frazzled, and not getting what you want.

We allow time to impact our self-worth. When we accomplish something or reach what we want within a certain time frame, *then* we allow ourselves to feel accepted and validated. When we don't achieve things, we beat ourselves up. *This* is the real issue we have with time. When we don't feel worthy of it or believe that it is even available to us, this ultimately stops us from evolving. Instead of never enough, we need to bask in the acceptance, peace, and gratitude of the abundance of time that keeps being given to us. That each morning, another bountiful beautiful day of our lives has been bestowed on us and *we ultimately have the choice of how we apply it to our lives.*

"The greatest gift you can give yourself is time."

— Oprah Winfrey

Being at Peace with Time

Knowing how to lean into time, respect it, and accept that it's about your relationship with it is ultimately how you will help curate your magnificent life. Most people don't spend time on themselves, but when we do - from a place of love, this is another step towards the freedom we so desire. Taking in the moment, appreciating the world around you, intentionally using your day, distinguishing between your *wants* and your *have-to's*, what's important or what's urgent, and forgiving yourself when you don't get it all done will fuel the life you crave. Time doesn't go fast or slow; it's the meaning you give to it that must change. It starts with allowing yourself to have time and see it in abundance. If you tell yourself you never have enough time, that is the reality you will create.

Calling Time on Our Relationship with Time

"All we have to decide is what to
do with the time that is given to us."

—J R R Tolkien

Life is precious. You are a divine and incredible being and should be having the time of your life, according to your heart and soul's desire.

Time *is* a sacred, precious resource that keeps on being given, and we are meant to use it on things that make us happy, fulfilled, and in alignment with our soul, instead of worrying about how much we have left. Then we are making the choice where we thrive every day, spending time doing what makes our soul sing, with those we love and adore the most, feeling connection, love, and support.

Supercharging Your Time

> ***"People who spend time wisely spend it on activities that advance their overall purpose in life."***
>
> ***—John C Maxwell***

One of the greatest gifts you can give yourself is to be present and accept that when you surrender to what it is you want, *everything* will be given to you with the right timing. When you focus on having a simpler, more discerning life, what's important will take you ever closer to freedom. Get clear on what you want, override that voice telling you it's not possible, and focus your energy on that. *That* is the best use of time.

How Do You Spend Your Time?

Investigate where you spend your time so you can shine a light on all the things that drain it. Are you intentional, knowing that you have time in abundance and that everything will work out for you at the right time? Or do you operate from not having enough, wasting time, procrastinating, feeling as if you're not using it productively, and scared of having it? Do you spend most of your time occupying yourself with things that distract you and stop you from feeling what you really feel? What might this be for you? Watching TV, gossiping with friends, ruminating about the past, worrying about the future, not being present, endlessly scrolling through social media, playing video games, shopping, snacking, drinking? Or do you spend your time doing things you consider "urgent" but not important such as checking notifications on your phone, thinking about what to do on the weekend or meeting with friends?

Believing you don't have enough time has benefits. It might make you feel important or in demand (but this is your ego talking). It's familiar, so it feels comfortable, but *you'll never grow whilst you stay in this place.* You might judge those that spend their time doing what they want and enjoy because you perceive it's not available to you. The real cost to believing you don't have enough time is that *you will not create what you want because you believe it's not available and you're not worthy of it.* You *must* tell yourself a different story.

You want to spend your time in *the zone*—the Dimension of Fulfilment, as Tony Robbins calls it. Where you do things that are important *and* meaningful to you. To live a life of abundance and purpose, *the focus of your commitment to doing those things in this zone must be where you want to spend your time.* What activities can you put in this zone? Look at your dream life statement, go back to those fifty things that make you happy. This is why you have to be so intentional. Otherwise, you'll spend all your time drifting around not feeling fulfilled.

Exercise

Keep challenging yourself by asking if you are using your time to the best of your ability? Are you doing things in alignment with your values? Activities you love? Essentially it comes down to a choice and whether you feel worthy of it. You do, just for being you.

Managing Procrastination

"A day can really slip by when you're deliberately avoiding what you're supposed to do."

— Bill Watterson

When you procrastinate, this isn't you thinking about what you want. Instead, you're thinking about what's painful, what you want to run away from—the change and unfamiliar territory that feels scary as you strive for the new you. When you revert to those things that already feel familiar to you, that you're competent at, it feels safe. So of course you're not going to follow through with it. Breaking your own promises just confirms the belief that you're not good enough or worthy enough to get what you want. Your subconscious will even go so far as to provide evidence to support that it was a good choice not to go chasing that job ("It wasn't the right one"), embark on a new relationship ("I'd get rejected anyway"), take up exercise ("Most people don't keep it up"), or finish a new course ("That's not going to really help me"). When we live from this place instead of making our dreams come true, we live with this internal conflict—we know what we want but don't understand why we can't get it.

"Only put off until tomorrow what you are willing to die having left undone."

— Pablo Picasso

Procrastination is not the same as being lazy or having poor time-management skills. It's something inside, holding you back from doing whatever you want to do. When you want to proactively make a change, *you have to see it as an investment of time* in yourself. Keep telling your brain a new story of the positive changes you've made. Maybe you fear achieving your dreams and desires because you don't know what's next. What happens then? Will you be rejected because you succeeded where others didn't? Will you still be approved of, loved, and accepted? Of course you will, and if anyone doesn't love or accept you, then they are not part of your epic level-up. What is really going on here that makes you self-sabotage and keeps you stuck?

Just start small and use your time wisely in the *Dimension of Fulfilment.* Recognise your progress, reward yourself, and practice gratitude as you magically push yourself out of your comfort zone.

Changing Your Mindset Around Time

Attaching timelines to what you want is okay, assuming they underpin your greatness. They should hold you accountable, push you forward, and help you grow. Schedule time to envision your greatness. There is a tipping point, however. When we get too rigid about how things have to look or how the outcome has to be, we don't operate from a place of truth, acceptance, and surrender. We operate from fear, trying not to lose control. Timelines *are not okay* when they feed into self-inflicted pressure and stress. All this does is deplete and contract you.

If you operate from a place of truth, expansion, and evolution, the universe will *always* give you the time you need to create what it is you want. Ultimately, if you are passionate about something, *you will always find time for it.* Time will expand or contract to the task you are doing. Be brave enough to slide the maybes and obligations off the table and start clearing the way for you to succeed in your ascension.

Positive Affirmations Around Time

Investigate why you have a negative attachment around time. Were you always rushed around as a child? Did you have parents who always seemed busy, run ragged, and had little time for themselves? Investigate it. Be curious. Challenge it. You need to rewire your programming with new stories—a positive loop of how you feel about time. Tell your brain you never lack time and you use it efficiently and effectively. Thus, you will slowly condition your mind to feel more present and relaxed with the time divinely given each day.

Being Deliberate with Use of Time

Be deliberate and intentional about how you use it, even if that means being very organised with your diary or blocking out chunks of time to use in a way that feels good to you. Otherwise, I guarantee distractions will happen and time will be lost.

Look at your day. Can you get up early to plan your day or do something that fills your cup? When can you schedule time to diligently journal, plan, read, meditate, and visualise? When can you block out time in your diary to do what you want to do? Where can you put boundaries in place to protect your time and energy so you can focus on what you want? Remind yourself that each time you let it slide, you're stepping further away from your magnificent life.

The first time you say no to things can be hard, but like anything else, it's a habit. A new story you need to tell yourself. *It's okay to say no*, or that you need time to yourself. Once you understand you won't be rejected, it's incredibly liberating to know you respect and honour yourself enough to set boundaries.

15

Living With Intention

"Something extraordinary happens
when you dramatically increase the focus, drive and
intention you bring to your life, work and relationships."

— Brendan Burchard

You've come such a long way—from discovering who you truly are, who you're not, and why you weren't experiencing the magnificence of a life you so desired, to aligning yourself with your truth to manifest the life of your dreams. You've armed yourself with tools, ideas, processes, and modalities to allow you to flourish into the incredible, abundant individual you were divinely designed to be. One who lives from their soul, from love, from source, the same energy as the universe itself.

You're now so sure of what you want because you care deeply about what *feels* right energetically. You know that living according to this authenticity will bring those wonderful feelings of freedom you seek, from a place of consciousness and in accordance with your absolute potential.

To achieve this, you *must* be intentional and deliberate about forging ahead. Being disciplined and focused on creating your freedom bridges the gap between where you are and creating the reality of your dreams. In every moment, choose how you want to feel, and make decisions from *that* place. When you keep redirecting energy back to the path on which you make decisions from *love*, you're bringing everything you want into your life because you're manifesting from your truth.

The Power of Choice

Your triumph and ultimate fulfilment in life is an inside job because this is what becomes your outside reality. It's you choosing to decide and having your "*why*" playing in the background, instead of that out-of-date, overplayed tape recorder. It's you telling yourself that you're not willing to settle for life *just happening to you, you're choosing one that happens for you.* The most important decision you can make is to *choose to experience an incredible life*. Say you no longer accept suffering and scarcity and instead focus your energy on the things that make you happy. Choose happiness, acceptance and fulfilment over validation and success and you'll be so much happier. Nothing external is going to give this to you.

Becoming Free

There is no need to go back to the old you—the one living from ego, conforming to what others think you should do—because that isn't truth. That's perception built on programming you know to be false. Your innate freedom to unleash your true self is already there, if you let it. You have limitless potent energy to express who you are deep down. Freedom comes from making decisions intuitively and what feels energetically right for the real authentic you.

"Great lives don't happen by default, they happen by design."

— Tony Robbins

The only way to become free and to live in truth is by adopting practices and foundations to help you evolve on your spiritual journey of awakening. I absolutely guarantee it will not happen otherwise. You must be deliberate and intentional about it, or else you'll find yourself straight back in that first stage. If you want to live an extraordinary life, *you have to live by design*. Detach yourself from the outcome and focus on the reasons *why* you're doing this. Let your purpose drive you to that incredible feeling of freedom. Behave in ways that feel good to your heart and soul, and your reality can only be blissful.

We Are All Unique

Find out what works for you and implement rituals and discipline. Just as learning to dance or play an instrument is a discipline with rules, techniques, and skills to be understood and perfected, so is curating the magnificent life you want. You don't have to be part of the "5 a.m. Club", but recognise what you need to do each day to fill up your needs. In turn, everyone else around you will light up, responding to your amazing, high-vibrational energy.

"The secret to your future is hidden in your daily routine. You have to be self-disciplined to spend your time wisely."

— Michelle Moore

Exercise

Fill up an entire A4 page with your self-care strategies—for example, positive affirmations, meditations, journaling, goal-setting strategies, rest, relaxation, fun, healthy food, personal development courses, studying, exercise, supplements, visualising, or self-awareness. Ask yourself (or ask the universe to demonstrate) how you can incorporate these into your day. What feels right? Where can you use your time more efficiently to invest in yourself? Should you do a quick meditation? Should you journal for twenty minutes? Can you listen to an audiobook in the car or while walking the dog? Just start asking so you can uncover what works for you.

Now look back at those original life domains. What is working, allowing you to ascend to empowerment and surrender, and what still needs growth? In which areas are you procrastinating or feeling stuck? What could you do more of and *why aren't you doing it?* Are there blocks still there? Are you addicted to the familiarity of this particular life area, even though you're not happy? Where can you be more deliberate in driving forward that area of your life that requires more direction?

Yes, it will feel uncomfortable, contrite, and even deluded and unreal as you consciously think new thoughts, visualise, and form new habits so different from your current existence. But this is a self-fulfilling prophecy. The more you focus and push through, the more you evolve and grow. The more you grow, the more rewarded you feel by what you're capable of creating, and the more motivated you will be to keep evolving and expanding into a conscious, authentic being. You *have* to tell your brain a different story than the default one human beings so often operate from. *It is golden on the other side*, and that feeling of joy and freedom is available to everyone.

"Everything you want is waiting for you to ask. Everything you want also wants you. But you have to take action to get it."

—Jack Canfield

The Four Pillars of Freedom

Michael Beckwith provides a framework which acts as a compass on your journey to freedom and peace in your soul.

First Pillar: Discipline

Primarily, you have to fall in love with discipline. Knowing that focus will bring joy helps you become disciplined. *Listen to yourself more often than not.* With every decision you make, put deliberate effort into doing an energetic check-up with yourself to ensure you're operating within the boundaries of what your inner soul wants. Be sure to acknowledge who is manning the ship here. Make yourself the priority of your interest, commitment, and love, which you then get to share with the world.

Most people think discipline means control, but those wanting to control things are often coming from a place of fear—of losing control or feeling life is against them, but it is the opposite. *Life is magnificent.* Discipline means you are making a choice, not control. It leans into freedom. *It means doing whatever it takes to wake up.* Make it a priority.

Second Pillar: Self-Responsibility

This means you can respond to the innate freedom in you. Listening to your true nature versus reacting to circumstance. Become a responder instead of a reactor. *High-functioning humans respond from love, whereas low functioning people react from fear.*

Each time you make a decision in any area of your life, ask if you're being responsible in the moment.

Third Pillar: Self-Awareness

This is you being aware of yourself, with no judgement. This is you "being whilst doing". This is pure growth and unfoldment. Be aware of the emotional content of your life and remain aware of your decision-making, your reactions, and your behaviour. You're just becoming aware of what's already there. With practice, there is more and more awareness of authenticity, less reactivity, and therefore more freedom. Bask in the contented feeling of becoming aware of what is already there, the truth inside.

How can you practice self-awareness in everything you do? Can you catch yourself when you get caught in the trap of fear, or are you operating from love?

Fourth Pillar: Self-Remembrance

Frequently remind yourself of your deep, unique soul expression. We are spiritual beings occupying a physical body, so let your soul drive you in all you do.

What can you do to always listen to your authentic self? Breathe? Be present? Remind yourself you are just energy, and your soul only wants you to live to your highest potential. Listen to *that* voice, not all the other ones you chose to hear.

The Importance of Intentionality

"The power of intention is the power to manifest, to create, to live a life of unlimited abundance and to attract into your life the right people at the right moments."

— Wayne Dyer

You start forming habits or rituals when you lay down intentions for how you want to live your life. Your intention allows you to focus. It provides the North Star, allowing you to navigate the direction of your life. Setting an intention means you are willing it to happen. It's about being patient with yourself, surrendering until you've realised you've gotten what you want. It is this vibration of willingness that helps set the direction of your life, so you can just flow. You are in control over every area of your life, *but it has to be intentional instead of automatic.*

Being intentional means you're living a life worth living—regardless of money, desires, relationships, and so on. It's available and already living in you now. How do you "intentionalise" your destiny? By feeling and emotionalising your experience. That's what our soul wants for us. To feel everything. *The only way you can curate an extraordinary life is to feel it. Otherwise, you just ignore it and push those feelings down. It's no longer about escaping it or distracting yourself from the things you don't want to feel.* You need to be present. As you fully experience life, you're no longer avoiding things or having repeated conversations in your head or playing out hypotheticals. Your vibe is clean, wide open, and intentional, so creation is open for you, and you consciously create your life every day.

Exercise

Write down or tell yourself a daily willing intention, and remind yourself of this frequently throughout the day (stick it on the fridge, notification on your phone, anywhere where you will deliberately see it).

For example:

Today I intend to be: kind to everyone around me, to be more receptive to the good that is happening in my life, to be thankful for everything I have, to know that I'm exactly where I need to be, and so on.

Rituals

Routines are just a ritual to live your life by. *This creates your habits, which create your behaviour, which creates your experience.* Human beings love rituals because they feel safe and predictable. They provide regulation, structure, and boundaries. This allows us to ascend to a place where the new conscious versions of ourselves become automatically self-aware and focused on creating our best lives. This is you cleverly manipulating the brain's default setting of automatic, living from consciousness and awareness so you calibrate up to the 2.0 version of you.

Using Rituals for Growth

Implementing rituals helps you remain disciplined on your path of expansive growth. We grow in two ways: pain or insight. When we are not consciously embracing our vision of life, we can only grow via pain. For example: "If I go out there, I'll be eaten by a sabre-toothed tiger", or "if I stick my hand in an oven, I'll get a burned hand". So we make choices that move us away from pain. As we establish ourselves and become comfortable with who we are, we begin to grow through insight and wisdom. We learn that *something isn't for us,* so we dare to choose something else. We become more receptive and available to new ways of doing things. This is spiritual and infinite. Every day, tell yourself that you are on a path of external growth—that you embrace change, development, and unfoldment.

Keep asking yourself how you can grow. How can you unleash the potential that's inside you?

Exercise

Think about an area that really matters to you. Write down what your life is really like in that area. Be specific. Then ask yourself what rituals put you there. What are you consistently doing that creates this? What is serving you? What isn't serving you? What do you really want in that area? What is your vision? You now have a starting point and can create momentum from here by implementing these into other parts of your life.

Frequency Foundations For Freedom (The Four Fs)

This is about creating a "foundation" for what you want to feel in life and shifting away from hoping or expecting things a certain way. The energy of Frequency Foundations is driven by *who you are, not what you are,* and having the confidence to lean into this. We are human "beings", not human "doings".

When you "expect" things a certain way, you're simply trying not to feel a certain way. What are you trying *not* to feel? Rejected, unheard, or ignored? Whereas the energy of a Frequency Foundation means you're feeling and acting in a way that resonates at the frequency you have set as a foundation—as if *you already have what you want.* Then it becomes so much easier to attract it into your life and you no longer fear it's all going to come crashing down. You already shower yourself with love and affection at all times, and because you're resonating at this frequency, you attract more of it in your life. It can be no other way.

You cannot set a Frequency Foundation for something *unless you are already doing it.* It is not possible to create the physical manifestation of what you want if you are energetically vibrating from a different place. You need to remain present and practice self-awareness. Don't be upset when you're triggered or not getting what you want. Ask yourself where you need to clear up. What needs to be healed? Always look back at yourself, discover the emotional voids, process them, and move on up.

Ask what your priorities are and how you want this part of your life to look? Who are you when you have what you want in this domain? What emotions would you have when you have what you want? Write it as if you already have it. Who do you know who embodies this?

You get what you want because you are aligned with *who you are.* Your soul and human body join as you become the person you were always designed to be. By knowing this, you can bridge the gap between where you are and where you want to be. It becomes bigger than the details, and nothing feels like hard work. You become a person who welcomes this into their life.

You must *step* into the energy and become the future version of yourself; otherwise, it feels forced. Look at your dream life and write frequency foundations for the different domains. Print them off and keep them in a file to read every day, making sure they align with your dream life. The more you read these, the more you think about them and embody them. Incorporate time in your day to deliberately think as if *you are this future vision.* This becomes the soundtrack of your mind. Work on the energy you want coming in first, pay attention to what is working and feel it to your core. Choose to feel it all, even when it's scary. This takes you closer to your vibe. Then the things on your list become easy. You become a different person, the version of you you knew was in there, the one that wanted to be found all along.

Other Ways to Stay in Your Vibe!

Instead of saying "I want" or "I wish" or "I hope", choose to say "I have" or "I am" or "I'm willing". Catch yourself in the moment.

Each day, focus on your intentions. If you are struggling to focus, just take a couple of minutes to sit quietly and get in the headspace. Before you can attract the good things in, create space and release first. Just sit and quietly ask for any interference to be released and say thank you for the universe wanting to help you. This becomes a way of life, like a contract you have with yourself. Do this each day. Feel the intention of what you want. You can easily ground and centre yourself to your inner guidance and reintegrate with your inner self. It is safe to come back to yourself. *Be intentional to be intuitive.*

Look at your vision board *every single day.* This will keep you focused on your intent. Add to it and write all the things you have manifested so far in a dedicated journal. Write down your desires and dreams and action plan so it is visible. This is a *must.* Put your board where you will see it, wherever you think it will have the maximum impact.

When you have the motivation and the taste of a better, more empowered life, you really start to believe in yourself. This seeps into other areas, and this creates abundance. This brings you the rewards you want—financial, livelihood, relationships. You feel driven and determined and you will create amazing things.

Keep writing all your dreams in your manifestation diary.

Timetable a weekly life-review meeting in your diary. Are you edging closer to what you really want?

Write a letter to yourself ten years from now. You're sitting in the most amazing place; your life has been incredible. Talk about the moment you shifted. Detail all your accomplishments, writing them all down as if they have happened. Do what feels right. What are you wearing? Where have you been on vacation? What are you doing for your business/career? What is your health like? Save this letter in a safe place where you can periodically read it. See if it still lights you up and makes you super excited.

Celebrate your successes. What will you do when you've created what you want? You need to reward yourself as you hit milestones along the way, and acknowledge your greatness so you keep driving forward. The only person that will praise you is you. Make sure you know just how awesome you are, because that is who your brain listens to.

When you live intentionally, life just becomes easier. Start listening to yourself and visualising every day. It feels incredible! This then becomes the new pattern of thinking. The action you do take won't feel like hard work; it just flows. It feels easy and aligned because it's your truth. You'll naturally want to work for something you love because this is your passion.

Conclusion

You are a person who owns their divinity, their authenticity, their voice, and their vision for what they want from the one precious life you've been given. Your life is uniquely yours, governed by the essence of who you are, the soul residing in your heart. With the tools, techniques, love, and respect woven throughout this book, you have become liberated from perception and instead make courageous choices that light the way to the feelings of freedom and joy you seek.

Life is a never-ending journey of unfoldment as you discover your truth and the path you were designed to walk. As you heal and calibrate up from the nonsense holding you back, life will reflect this back to you, as if by magic. You will ascend into who you were always designed to be—a limitless, potent, joyful, peaceful, powerful co-creator with the universe as you unleash the power inside of you to create the magnificent life of your dreams. Your self-esteem skyrockets as does your self-acceptance, worthiness, compassion and love for yourself. No longer do you feel dragged through life by the trappings of your ego. Instead, you bravely attach yourself to the strings of your heart.

Give yourself the permission to step into your power instead of shrinking down to be someone that isn't you. Don't be afraid of being you, of making mistakes or following your true path. Return home to where you're meant to be—that vibration of love—the one you were born at. It means you showing up, reminding yourself of why you're doing this and the consequences of not. It's listening to the divine energy inside and trusting yourself in every decision you make.

Now you're awake, you can never go back to sleep.

You can't unsee what you've seen.

Even when you can't see what you want, trust that it's in the "unseen", and soon it will become visible.

Surrender, trust, and have faith that life will always provide the answers as long as you're willing to listen. This book is just the start. Don't you ever dare look back with regret.

So what's stopping you? You create your reality, and it is perfect because you are too. You are complete, whole, loved, and have the innate power inside to create the life of your dreams—that's all creation wants for you.

With love and gratitude,

Di

Acknowledgments

Thank you to Keith Gordon and the editors at Duo Storytelling, Susan Friedman at Aviva Publishing, Shiloh Schroeder at Fusion Creative Works, and Marta Suchomska. Thank you to my coaches Sanae Floyd, Sara Longoria, Christine Gail, Judi Thureson and Michelle Bloem for the many discoveries and teachings I have learnt. Thank you to the beautiful people and friends across the world who support and uplift me on my journey so I can consciously uplift others—namely Jacey Graham, Laurie Jimerson, and Chérie Carstens Petersen. I love you all. Thank you for believing in me.

Thank you to my family who support me and allow me to effortlessly feel love. You are the source of my greatest joy and also my greatest teachers. You soften the edges and show me what life is truly about—that the vibration of love is all that matters.

List of Citations

1. Lipton, Bruce. The Biology of Belief (March 2005).
2. Hendricks, Gay. The Big Leap (April 2009).
3. Tseng, J., Poppenk, J. Brain meta-state transitions demarcate thoughts across task contexts exposing the mental noise of trait neuroticism. Nat Commun 11, 3480 (2020).
4. Lashley, K. S. The behavioristic interpretation of consciousness. I. *Psychological Review, 30*(4) (1923): 237–272.
5. Lally, Phillippa et al. "How are habits formed: Modelling habit formation in the real world." *European Journal of Social Psychology* 40 (2010): 998-1009.
6. http://www.greatergood.berkeley.edu
7. Toussaint, Loren. "Forgiveness, Stress, and Health: a 5-Week Dynamic Parallel Process Study." Luther College (2016).
8. Luskin, F . Forgive for Good: A Proven Prescription for Health and Happiness. New York, NY: HarperCollins (2002).
9. Cornish, Marilyn A., and Nathaniel G. Wade. "A therapeutic model of self forgiveness with intervention strategies for

counselors." Journal of Counseling & Development 93.1 (2015): 96-104.

10. Mills, Paul J., et al. "The role of gratitude in spiritual well-being in asymptomatic heart failure patients." *Spirituality in clinical practice* 2.1 (2015): 5.

11. Huffman, Jeff C., et al. "Design and baseline data from the Gratitude Research in Acute Coronary Events (GRACE) study." *Contemporary clinical trials* 44 (2015): 11-19.

12. Huffman, Jeff C., et al. "Feasibility and utility of positive psychology exercises for suicidal inpatients." *General hospital psychiatry* 36.1 (2014): 88-94.

13. Lambert, Nathaniel M., et al. "A changed perspective: How gratitude can affect sense of coherence through positive reframing." *The Journal of Positive Psychology* 4.6 (2009): 461-470.

14. Liang, Hongyu, et al. "Mediating effects of peace of mind and rumination on the relationship between gratitude and depression among Chinese university students." *Current Psychology* (2018): 1-8.

15. Updegraff, John A., Roxane Cohen Silver, and E. Alison Holman. "Searching for and finding meaning in collective trauma: results from a national longitudinal study of the 9/11 terrorist attacks." *Journal of personality and social psychology* 95.3 (2008): 709.

16. Wood, Alex M., et al. "Gratitude influences sleep through the mechanism of pre-sleep cognitions." *Journal of psychosomatic research* 66.1 (2009): 43-48.

17. Berg, Jodi L. "The Role of Personal Purpose and Personal Goals in Symbiotic Visions" (April 2015).

18. Snodgrass, J.G., Asiaghi, A. The pictorial superiority effect in recognition memory. *Bull. Psychon. Soc.* 10, 1–4 (1977).

19. Whitehouse, Andrew JO, Murray T. Maybery, and Kevin Durkin. "The development of the picture superiority effect." *British Journal of Developmental Psychology* 24.4 (2006): 767-773.

20. Paivio, A., Csapo, K. Short-term sequential memory for pictures and words. *Psychon Sci* 24, 50–51 (1971).

Made in USA - Kendallville, IN
45133_9781636181714
07.14.2022 1408